Advance Praise for

In this highly readable book Jud s. mattered in his life. In doing so he causes the reader to reflect on what matters in the reader's life. I recommend it to people regardless of where they are in their journey of life.

—Sanford R. Beckett
Retired Associate Director
NorthStar Church Network: An Association of Baptist Congregations

In *Panning for Gold*, pastor and author Judson Edwards shares the joy and enrichment that comes from discovering what really matters in life. In his own poetic style, Edwards sifts through a lifetime of memories and gives us insightful nuggets of everyday wisdom gleaned through years of pastoral experience. From such items as God and Scripture, to music and laughter, and sports and writing, Edwards shares in a refreshing way, experiences and truths that enlighten and nourish the soul. It is a delightful read and his practical wisdom and honesty challenge us to evaluate the priorities of everyday life.

—W. Merlin Merritt
Author of *Seeing the Son on the Way to the Moon*

In *Panning for Gold*, Jud Edwards looks all the way back and mines the deep treasures of his reflective life. He asks, "Of the myriad experiences I've had—happy and sad, uplifting and debilitating, exhilarating and normal, what really mattered?" It's hard to distinguish the best parts of this book, for each chapter contains a gem or two distilled from the author's lifelong reflecting. For instance, I was moved by his account of how "justice matters" in the real world of today—of how walls need to be replaced with bridges. Readers will immediately identify with Edwards' genuine honesty shining through each of eighteen chapters— the real gold he has collected as a lifelong panhandler.

—William R. Hornbuckle
Retired music minister

Smyth & Helwys Publishing, Inc.
6316 Peake Road
Macon, Georgia 31210-3960
1-800-747-3016

(Unless otherwise noted, all Scripture references are from the New Revised Standard Version, 1989.)

Library of Congress Cataloging-in-Publication Data

Names: Edwards, Judson, author.
Title: Panning for gold : looking back on a life of joy / by Judson
Edwards.
Description: Macon, GA : Smyth & Helwys Publishing, 2021. | Includes
bibliographical references.
Identifiers: LCCN 2021042115 | ISBN 9781641733373 (paperback)
Subjects: LCSH: Edwards, Judson. | Baptists--Clergy--Biography. | Christian
life--Baptist authors. | Joy--Religious aspects--Christianity.
Classification: LCC BX6495.E3555 A3 2021 | DDC 253/.7--dc23
LC record available at https://lccn.loc.gov/2021042115

PANNING FOR
GOLD

Looking Back on a Life of Joy

Yours for gold,

Judson Edwards

JUDSON EDWARDS

Also by Judson Edwards

A Matter of Choice

Running the Race

With Love, From Dad

Dancing to Zion

Regaining Control of Your Life

What They Never Told Us about How to Get Along with Each Other

The Leadership Labyrinth

Hidden Treasures

Making the Good News Good Again

Blissful Affliction

Quiet Faith

Bugles in the Afternoon

Contents

Introduction

Robert Browning began his poem "Rabbi Ben Ezra" with this invitation: "Grow old along with me, the best is yet to be; the last of life for which the first was made." As I have slowly crept toward old age, I have at times wondered if the poet really knew what he was talking about. Growing older has been a mixed blessing, to say the least.

On the negative side, old age has given me some of the telltale symptoms of aging—bad knees, thinning hair, occasional memory lapses, lower back issues, and an increasing list of minor health problems. For most of my life, I took no pills and never went to the doctor. Now, I take six pills every night and visit my doctors far more than I desire.

But growing older has had a positive side as well. It has afforded me free time in retirement that I never had when I worked full-time. I now have time to read, take a long walk every morning, leave town whenever I want to, leisurely peruse the morning newspaper and sip several mugs of coffee, visit with my kids and grandkids, and spend fun days with Sherry, my wife of fifty years. I sometimes say to Sherry, "I'm pretty sure we're living the good life." And I'm absolutely certain that we are.

I've also discovered that one of the enjoyable facets of aging is being able to reflect on my life and realize how blessed I've been. When I look back on my life, I'm filled with gratitude. If I was going to have an epitaph on a gravestone, I would choose this one: *Blessed beyond Measure.* When I tally up the experiences of seventy years of life, the positive ones far outnumber the negative ones. I realize that not everyone can say this, and I'm grateful that I can.

Growing older has also given me the opportunity to reflect on my life and see what has really mattered. Jesus once asked a probing question in Mark 8:36: "What will it profit us if we gain the whole world and lose our own soul?" That question raises the frightful possibility that we can invest our lives in things that don't matter. In an attempt to gain the whole world, we can end up losing our soul. We can invest in the wrong things and hear those sad words originally addressed to the rich fool in Jesus' famous parable: "You fool! This very night your life is being demanded of you. And the things you have prepared, whose will they be?" (Luke 12:20).

I suppose this book is, in a way, a trip down memory lane. It gives me the opportunity to look back at my life and try to discern what has really mattered. It also gives me the opportunity to tell my family and friends—and you, the reader—what has made my life such a rewarding journey.

I claim no particular expertise in the art of living. I've made more than my share of mistakes, taken more than one wrong turn, and am regularly reminded of how much I *don't* know. I've just been privileged to live seventy years and learn a few things along the way. Consider these pages, perhaps, not as the pontifications of a guru who has discovered the meaning of life but as the random musings of someone who simply knows he has been blessed beyond measure.

A few years ago, I occasionally took my four grandsons to a local miniature golf course. They enjoyed playing miniature golf, but they also liked the panning-for-gold feature at the golf place. For a small fee, they could dip a pan in a man-made stream and catch some glittering rocks as they floated by. It wasn't real gold they were catching, but they didn't care. They could take home with them a small pouch bulging with sparkling rocks—pyrite, quartz, obsidian, and others—and show them to their parents.

I decided to title this book *Panning for Gold* because what I plan to do in these pages is something like what my grandsons did at that miniature golf place. I want to sift through a lifetime of memories as they float by and catch the ones that are the brightest and best. Out of all the experiences and truths that have come my way, I want to grab the ones that have mattered most, put them in these pages, and share them with you.

I can't guarantee that there is any gold in this book. But maybe there is at least a shiny rock or two that you will find worth keeping.

Chapter 1

God Matters
Taking a Sacred Journey

*You shall love the Lord your God with all your heart,
and all your soul, and with all your mind. This is the
greatest and first commandment.* —Jesus of Nazareth

When I was seven years old, I went forward at the end of a worship service at the Westview Baptist Church in Houston and told our pastor that I had invited Jesus into my heart and wanted to be baptized. Several weeks later, I was baptized during one of our worship services and remember feeling both pride and relief. I was proud that I had done something difficult, something God wanted me to do. But I was also relieved that the baptism was behind me. I didn't really enjoy being in the limelight, and I was glad I wouldn't have to do it again.

That decision those many years ago launched me on a lifetime journey of trying to know, love, and serve God. Looking back on it now, that decision set me on a path that was uncommonly religious.

Even as a child, I tried to read the Bible every day, go to church every time the doors were open, pray every night before bed, and be a Christian witness to my friends. This eventually led me to tell my high school classmates that I couldn't go to our senior prom because, as a Christian, I didn't dance. When I look back on my growing-up years, I see a boy trying desperately to please God. I also see a boy who maybe wasn't quite as carefree and joyful as he should have been.

That desire to know, love, and serve God has never left me though, and has been the motivating factor in my life. It has prompted me not only to skip my senior prom but to major in religion at college; decide that God was calling me to preach, go to seminary, and become a pastor for thirty-eight years; write an assortment of Christian books; and define myself first and foremost as a follower of Jesus.

I've moved through stages and steps all along the way and am now a different kind of Christian from what I was even ten years ago. I assure myself that this is exactly what is supposed to happen on a spiritual journey, that we are not to be at age seventy where we were at twenty or thirty. There is a reason we call our relationship with God a "walk," a "journey," or a "pilgrimage"—we're supposed to be *moving*. When I try to trace some of the ways I have moved, I realize that my understanding of God has transitioned through at least four phases.

A Demanding God

For much of my early life, God was demanding and even punitive. One reason I did all of those religious things as a child and skipped my senior prom was to keep at bay the wrath of God. At church I heard terrifying sermons about hell and the punishment awaiting people who didn't know and obey God.

I also heard sermons about the second coming of Christ, all stressing the horror of being left behind. I still remember one of the songs we sang in our youth group about the second coming: "Life was filled with guns and wars, and everyone got trampled on the floor. I wish we'd all been ready. There's no time to change your mind. The Son has come . . . and you've been left behind."

I certainly wanted to meet Jesus gladly, should he return in my lifetime, so I worked overtime to be ready. Every Sunday, I took an offering envelope to Sunday school with me. The envelope had boxes I could check to verify if I had performed a series of religious duties. Had I studied my Sunday school lesson? Check. Had I brought my Bible to church? Check. Had I done my daily Bible readings all week? Check. Was I staying for the worship service? Check. Had I enclosed an offering in the envelope? Check. If I checked all the boxes, I was a 100-percent Christian, and that was my goal every week.

The problem with this approach to God is that it doesn't have much joy in it. It is brimming with *obligation* but sorely lacking in *celebration.* People who serve God out of fear don't laugh a whole lot. They also tend to burn out, and even if they don't burn out, they make the people around them miserable. When our goal in life is to be a 100-percent Christian, we tend to expect other people to have the same goal. And when they don't, or can't, we blast them with either condescension or condemnation. That's why most people would much rather be around a happy pagan than a Christian striving for perfection.

But for much of my early life, God was a taskmaster, wanting me to toe the line and check all the boxes. I did my dead-level best to be a model Christian and received a lot of praise for my serious devotion to God. But, as far as I can remember, no one ever had to tell me to be quiet and quit laughing so much.

A Gracious God

It was while I was at seminary that I began to get a new understanding of God. That understanding came more from the books I read than from the classes I took. I started to read Keith Miller and Bruce Larson and their ideas about the emerging church. I discovered Robert Capon and Frederick Buechner and their ideas about the radical grace of God. I read Karl Olsson's book *Come to the Party* and was astonished that anyone would liken the Christian life to a party.

I had always thought of the church as an army and Christians as soldiers of the cross. What I was reading was new and exciting and filled with grace. God was *for* me? God wanted to bless me? God wanted me to dance, not march? Maybe there was a reason the first Christians called their message the good news!

One section in *Come to the Party* nailed me perfectly:

> Some time in the summer of 1967, I came face to face with the real me and suddenly discovered the simple but overwhelming fact which I had preached and written about for thirty years—that we are justified by faith alone and not by works, "lest any man should boast." What that meant for *me*, quite practically, was that God has already accepted the real *me* in Christ and that it was okay to be that *me*. I did not have to overlay that *me* with any sweat-soaked

slave shirt of my own. I did not have to be a professional prelate, preacher, president, pundit, professor, Protestant, or anything else to make it with God . . . I was free to be me and to be human.[1]

When you've spent your whole life checking boxes and striving for perfection, that is awfully good news. I discovered the liberating truth in 1 John 4:19: "We love because he first loved us." God loved us *first*, before we ever prayed, worshiped, witnessed, tithed, or did any other religious deed. We don't have to earn God's love . . . because we already have it! Like Karl Olsson, I came to see that I was free to be me and to be human. I came to see God as full of grace, and that truth has been the core of my faith ever since.

A Mysterious God

The older I get the more mysterious God becomes. When I was a pastor, I always felt pressure to answer people's questions about God, the Bible, and all things related to faith. After all, I was a paid and trained religious professional, someone supposedly filled with biblical knowledge, someone who talks to God every day. If I didn't know the answer to people's questions about spiritual things, who did? It is almost impossible for a pastor to say, "I don't know."

Maybe it's because I'm now retired and not on the firing line, but I no longer feel that I have to know the answers to the great mysteries of life. I don't know why bad things happen to good people. I don't know why God is so silent. I don't know what will happen to people after they die. I don't know how to interpret some of the strange, even violent, passages in the Bible. I don't know a really winsome way to do Christian evangelism. I don't know how or why prayer works.

I don't know a lot of things and no longer feel the pressure to pretend that I do. There is great relief in letting God be God and trusting in divine sovereignty. I sometimes wonder if our Christian witness to the world wouldn't be more effective if we Christians would all take a vow of honesty and admit our ignorance about God, the Bible, and eternity.

---

1. Karl Olsson, *Come to the Party* (Waco: Word Books, 1972), 46–47.

When we resort to simplistic formulas and three-point sermons, ordinary people can't relate to our oversimplifications. They know that we're not being honest, and they also know that they haven't experienced reality the way we're describing it. When we make everything black and white in a world that most people experience as gray, we Christian witnesses simply don't have much credibility. Do we really want a God we can understand and explain? Or do we want—or maybe need—a God who is so awesome and incomprehensible that we stand in tongue-tied awe before that God?

That's the way it was for the Jews in the Old Testament. They were so awestruck by Yahweh that they wouldn't speak Yahweh's name. We, on the other hand, are so familiar with God that He is the Man Upstairs, and we can explain God to the world in four spiritual laws.

The older I get, the more comfortable I become with the wide gulf fixed between the human and the divine. I'm content to let God be God, admit my vast ignorance, and lean, with all the faith I have, into the loving sovereignty of this mysterious God. I don't have to be the answer man anymore. I can be a grateful pilgrim, fascinated by and faithful to God the Ultimate Mystery.

An Incarnate God

The New Testament writers are unanimous in telling us that this Ultimate Mystery became visible for a brief time in human history. They tell us a seemingly preposterous truth: when Jesus came into the world for about thirty years, we humans got to see God. John put it like this: "And the Word became flesh and lived among us, and we have seen his glory, the glory as of a father's only son, full of grace and truth" (John 1:14).

In his letter to the Colossian church, Paul calls Jesus "the image of the invisible God" (Col 1:15a). For the biblical writers, this truth was both astonishing and life-transforming. After they met Jesus, their lives were changed forever. Unlike them, I've never had a face-to-face encounter with Jesus, but I do know that I've never found anyone in history as compelling as Jesus of Nazareth. If God is like Jesus, then I have to say I'm crazy about God.

We could spend a lifetime, for instance, just trying to under-stand and live Jesus' Sermon on the Mount. I'm addressing in this book what really matters, but Jesus addressed that topic far more eloquently and effectively in the Sermon on the Mount than I can even hope to do. If you truly want to know what really matters, read Matthew 5, 6, and 7. Jesus' effort makes mine look trite and foolish. In the sermon, he deals with the gut-level issues we all have to face—happiness, influence, anger, adultery, getting along with people, loving our enemies, prayer, investing our money, worry, loving God, and more. In three short chapters, Jesus lays out for us the things that really matter and what it means to follow him.

If all Jesus had given us was the brilliance of that sermon, his contribution to the world would have been enormous. But that is just a small sample of what he offered the world. Watch the way he relates to people. Watch him confront the religious bureaucracy of his day. Listen to his simple but profound parables. See the way he seeks out the last, the least, and the lost. Watch him die on that cross outside the city of Jerusalem. See him escape the tomb and seek out his heartbroken friends.

There has never been anyone, for me at least, more inspiring than Jesus. And whenever I get frustrated that God seems so incompre-hensible and inscrutable, I take comfort in this: God is just like Jesus, and therefore I am in good hands.

I mentioned earlier that I've transitioned through these four concepts of God, but I'm not sure that's the most accurate way to express my spiritual journey. It would probably be more truthful to say that these four concepts of God have all been a part of that journey—and still are.

I still have a demanding God who calls me to be better than I am.

I still have a gracious God who loves me relentlessly in spite of myself.

I still have a mysterious God who baffles me and leaves me speechless.

And I still have a God who speaks to me most eloquently and forcefully in the person of Jesus the Christ.

In his book *The Truing of Christianity*, John Meagher writes that "faith is especially dedicated to the cherishing of what is true."[2] Those of us who are on personal journeys with God are dedicated to what is true and praying that our lives are pursuing Truth, dedicated to Truth, and loving Truth.

If we can do that, those spiritual journeys will make us better versions of ourselves. Gradually, or maybe dramatically, we will become a new person. No one knew that better than the apostle Paul who had his life transformed by Christ and testified, "So if anyone is in Christ, there is a new creation: everything old has passed away; see, everything has become new" (2 Cor 5:17).

Later in *The Truing of Christianity*, Meagher writes about the difference a God-oriented focus makes in a person's life:

> You can recognize the smell of a good life when you come across it, whatever your criteria for spotting the symptoms. Perhaps you are struck when you find freedom from irritability, a steady brightness of the eyes, the easy physical grace that expresses mindfulness, attitudes of capacious generosity, laconic simplicity of expression, remarkable poise in the midst of adversity, a gracious readiness to endure real hurts without resentment—whatever your checklist may be, you have your ways of identifying those, both the living and the long gone, who have realized some of the public secrets that are clearly worth knowing and embodying. The strong tendency of such lives to be associated with God is a matter of public record. If the state of your faith is skeptical or insecure about the desirability of Godwardness, check the evidence.[3]

In short, a genuine journey with God changes us, makes us better people, imbues us with the smell of a good life, and leads us to truth and genuineness. A Godward life, intent on knowing, serving, and loving God, *matters*.

---

2. John Meagher, *The Truing of Christianity* (New York: Doubleday, 1990), 39.

3. Meagher, *Truing*, 215.

Chapter 2

Family Matters
Loving Up Close and Personal

Happiness is having a large, loving, caring, close-knit family in another city. —George Burns

All of us find ourselves in a network of relationships not of our own choosing. We live in a web of family relationships that, to a large degree, determines who we become. The irony in this situation is that this all-important web of relationships is truly not of our own choosing. We don't get to pick our families; we're just born into the world with a mother and father, brothers and sisters, perhaps, and other extended family members too numerous to mention.

Then, we get to spend the rest of our lives relating to these people. We didn't choose them, but they bear our last name or our bloodline, and, like it or not, we're stuck with them for a lifetime. They will determine what we look like, what language we speak, what foods we eat, what sports we play, what church we attend, and what music we enjoy. They will, to a large extent, determine who we are, how we feel about ourselves, and whether or not we're happy or sad. For better or worse, we will forever bear their stamp on our lives.

Some people get to be born into families that are healthy, happy, and harmonious. I was one of those people, and when I look back on my family, I am filled with gratitude. When I take a long look at the past and think about my grandparents, parents, aunts, uncles, cousins, and others who were my family as I was growing up, I have overwhelmingly positive memories. I remember festive Christmases, birthday parties, ball games, Halloween trips through the neighborhood, singing together in living rooms, sitting together in church, eating sumptuous meals at the family table, and generally celebrating life with a network of people who loved me.

When I zoom in closer and look at my family now, I can only consider myself among all people most blessed. A wife whom I have loved for fifty years. A daughter and a son who have always been the pride of my life. Four grandsons who, as Garrison Keillor used to say about the people in Lake Wobegon, are way above average. A brother and sister to whom I am still close. In-laws, nephews, and nieces who are delightful. I have a treasure chest of loving relationships in my immediate family now, and there's not one in the bunch I would like to swap in for a better model. So I'm one of the blessed ones, born into a loving, supportive family that has sustained me all of my days.

But I also know that not everyone can make that claim. As a pastor, I worked with families for years who were anything *but* loving and supportive. Some people have the misfortune of being born into families that are abusive, negligent, cold, crazy, or dysfunctional in some other way. For them, family is not something to be *embraced* but *escaped*. And when they look back on their family heritage, they don't count their blessings; they count their scars.

One thing is certain, though: families *matter*. They either bring us joy or sorrow, but they most definitely shape our lives. We are who we are because of our families. And our children and grandchildren are who they are because of the family environment we're providing for them every day. Our goal is to make sure that environment is life-giving and full of joy. When I think of the qualities that will bring life and joy to families, three specific ones come immediately to mind.

The first one is *fun*. Families should have a lot of fun. They should laugh a lot. They should look for ways to bless and delight one another. When I was growing up, my parents brought the sports page and a cup of hot tea to my bedside every morning. I just assumed all kids got treated that way. I was in middle school before I realized I was the only one getting that kind of royal treatment. Some might hear this and want to say I was spoiled or pampered, but I prefer to say I was blessed. What a fun way to start every day! It was a simple way for my parents to tell me I was special and deserving of their best attention.

Family life is not supposed to be drudgery; it's supposed to be fun. When our kids were growing up, we put a Nerf basketball hoop over a door in the living room of our house. Visitors looked at it with interest, puzzled as to why a basketball goal was part of our living room décor. It was there because we had almost daily games of "H-O-R-S-E" or "21." Those games were competitive and heated, and as I recall, I took my family to the cleaners on a regular basis. I developed an underhanded "Granny" shot that was almost unbeatable. Sherry, Stacy, and Randel don't remember the outcome of our games exactly the way I do, but I'm pretty sure I was the family champ. One thing we all agree on: those games sure were fun.

When I retired and we moved to the Austin area to be closer to Stacy and Randel and their families, one of the first things we did in our new home was install a Nerf basketball hoop in the front hallway. Now the grandsons play Nerf basketball with us—and regularly get smoked by the same underhanded "Granny" shot that took down their parents.

What I have come to see is that the world is often a sad and somber place. Our parents and grandparents live in that sad and somber world. So do our brothers and sisters, children and grandchildren. We need to do everything in our power to have fun in our families, to provide for our families a place of joy and laughter. We need to deliver them the sports page and hot tea in the morning and play Nerf basketball with them every chance we get.

When our children and grandchildren look back on their lives one day as I'm doing now, they will probably not celebrate the advice we gave them, the chores they had to perform, or the trips to church every Sunday. But they just might celebrate things like hot tea in the morning and Nerf basketball games.

The second quality we can foster in our families is *freedom*. As difficult as it might be, I think we have to grant our family members the freedom to be who *they* choose to be, not who *we* want them to be. And trust me, that will be difficult from time to time. Our parents might make some choices we don't agree with. Our siblings might choose a life path very different from our own. Our children might decide not to become clones of us and, at some point, to take off on a road less traveled. And our grandchildren are growing up in a world so different from the one we grew up in that we hardly know the ground rules anymore. So let's not try to be the grand orchestrators of other people's lives.

That is much easier said than done. When you love someone as much as we love these people in our family, it's hard not to offer advice and give wise counsel. We see these loved ones approaching a cliff and feel we must warn them of their coming catastrophe. Why can't they see what we can see? Why do they want to ruin their lives when they have such a great resource as you and me to rescue them? And why do they resent our well-meaning attempts to help?

When I was a pastor, I occasionally dealt with families in some kind of crisis. Often, the issue of freedom was at the heart of this family turmoil. A woman was upset at her mother for wanting to remarry a man less than a year after the woman's father had died. A football coach was distraught and angry because his son confided to him that he was homosexual. A father was fuming because his high school son got an earring. Parents were at odds with their daughter over the college she should attend.

These were serious, family-threatening crises to these people, and the issue of freedom was at the heart of them all. But even a little reflection would show that denying those family members their freedom was probably not a wise idea. In every case, those upset people might win the battle . . . and lose the war.

The daughter might convince her mother not to remarry . . . and then have to live with a lonely, bitter parent. The coach might denounce his son's sexual orientation . . . and then be alienated from him forever. The father might ban his son's earring . . . but at what price? And the parents might forbid their daughter from attending the college of her choice . . . and have to live with a daughter who thinks they made her settle for second best.

The truth is, people are free. Free to remarry. Free to declare their sexual orientation. Free to wear an earring. Free to choose the college they want to attend. And even if those people are our beloved family members and we feel they're making a big mistake, it's usually counterproductive to usurp their freedom and try to assume control of their lives.

Certainly, children need structure, training, and discipline. Parents and grandparents need to offer guidance and wisdom to their offspring. And we can offer kind and thoughtful words of counsel to the people we love. But we should always do so with the awareness that these people are free to become who they want to be. They don't have to dress like us, attend our church, listen to our music, vote our party, or heed our advice.

We'd like to think that if they were smart, they would. They would look at our exemplary lives and want to become just like us. But they don't have to. They're free to take a different road of their own choosing and follow that road wherever it takes them.

The third quality is *forgiveness*. When the Bible says "all have sinned and fall short of the glory of God" (Rom 3:23), I'm pretty sure that includes you and me and everyone in our families. We will all sin and fall short of the glory of God. Our parents will make mistakes. Our brothers and sisters will go astray. Our kids will embarrass us. And our grandkids will make us shake our heads in bewilderment. If we have this idea that we're going to have the first family in history with no skeletons in the closet, we're in for a rude awakening. Eventually, we all come face to face with the reality that Romans 3:23 applies to us and our family.

Tragically, some people deal with this reality by becoming a "trading stamp family." Years ago, there were things called trading stamps in America. Grocery stores would award shoppers a certain number of trading stamps based on the size of their grocery bill. Shoppers would paste these stamps into redemption books and eventually take them to a redemption center to pick out a gift. When I was newly married, I remember going with Sherry to an S&H Green Stamp redemption center and coming home with a new toaster.

Some families choose to save up hurts and grudges like trading stamps and eventually cash them in. The husband remembers his wife's cutting words and lets them fester. The wife remembers her husband's insensitive act and won't let that memory go. The parents hold on to their son's drinking at the college party and refuse to trust him again. The daughter resents her parents' attempts to make her into a debutante and can't get past that resentment.

We can all fill in the blanks as to the ways our families have wounded us. And some of those wounds are still pretty tender. So we save up our stamps and one day decide to cash them in. We file for divorce, kick the kid out of the house, refuse to speak to our sibling, quit calling our parents, or in some other way do damage to our family system. We have finally collected enough stamps that we feel justified in cashing them in. Take a look at the current scene in our country: the pile of cashed-in redemption books is staggering.

But there is a better, more grace-full way to deal with these hurts. We can try to forgive. We can remember that all of us have sinned and fallen short of the glory of God and try to extend grace to our family members. We can decide to get out of the trading-stamp business and into the forgiving-family-members business.

It might not be easy, because grace and forgiveness are never easy. But we might be amazed at how much better we start to feel. Carrying those redemption books with us all the time is exhausting. The families that make it and survive these stressful times have short memories. They don't hold grudges, and they don't collect trading stamps. There might be some family actions and abuses that are beyond forgiveness, but they are few and far between. Most of the time, the problem is not the sin; it's our unwillingness to forgive that sin.

As I look back at what I've just written, it seems a bit "gimmicky" and "preachy." I'm afraid I've just offered you a nifty, three-point sermon titled "The Three F's of Family Fulfillment." I think maybe I've been a Baptist preacher for too many years. Forgive me.

No family's life is really that simple, and there's no formula for making families healthy and whole. But I think all of us would agree that our families matter. For better or worse, we're all shaped by our families, and it's almost impossible to overstate their importance. We are who we are, largely, because of the families that molded us. And the future of our children and grandchildren depends, in large measure, on the families in which they live.

So have fun. Give freedom. Learn to forgive. And see what happens.

Chapter 3

Sports Matter
Finding a Reason to Cheer

Sports teaches you character. It teaches you to play by the rules. It teaches you what it feels like to win and lose. It teaches you about life. —Billie Jean King

As a boy, I had a clear idea of where my life was heading. I was either going to become a shortstop in the big leagues like my hero, Luis Aparicio, or I was going to become a running back in the NFL like my hero, Ronnie Bull. Either way, I was going to be a famous sports star. After all, I had made the all-stars playing shortstop on my Little League baseball team. And I was the starting running back on my Little League football team. It was fairly obvious to everyone, I thought, that I was bound for some kind of hall of fame.

That fantasy had a shocking collision with reality one Saturday morning at a high school track meet. I was a sophomore sprinter for the Spring Woods Tigers, entered at that meet in the 100-yard dash. As I set my starting blocks, I looked at the lane next to me and saw a runner who was built like a linebacker. I weighed 130 pounds; he must have weighed 210. He certainly didn't look like any sprinter I had ever seen.

"Don't worry," I assured myself. "This is about speed not strength. He might beat me in arm-wrestling, but that doesn't mean he can outrun me." Well, to put it bluntly, he could . . . and did. That behemoth beside me took off like a rocket when the gun sounded and beat me to the finish line by a good 10 yards. As I recall, he ran a 9.6, and I ran a 10.6. When you get beat by 10 yards in a 100-yard race, you've not just been beaten; you've been embarrassed.

But that race got me thinking: if there are people in this world who outweigh me by 80 pounds and can beat me by 10 yards in a 100-yard dash, I might not be the elite athlete I think I am. After that track meet, I started seriously considering the possibility that I might need to reimagine my future.

I later learned that the runner whose dust I was eating that day was Norm Bulaich. He became a star football player at TCU, a number one draft pick in the pro draft, and had a ten-year career as a running back in the NFL. As it turned out, there was no shame in getting beat by someone like Norm Bulaich. But it did give me a strong and painful taste of reality. The truth was: 9.6/210 Norm Bulaich might one day make the pros. 10.6/130 Jud Edwards? Not a chance.

But, in spite of that painful encounter with reality, I never soured on sports. I mentioned in the last chapter that my parents brought me the sports page in bed every morning, and I have faithfully read the sports page every morning since. My mornings now begin with several cups of coffee and reading the sports pages from the *Austin American-Statesman* and the *San Antonio Express-News*. But reading about sports every morning is just one small part of my fixation on all things athletic.

When my children were growing up, they both played a number of sports, and Sherry and I traveled all over the Houston area watching Stacy and Randel play baseball, volleyball, football, and basketball, and run track. Now that we have four grandsons, we're getting to travel all over the Austin area watching them play baseball, football, basketball, and lacrosse. To read about sports in the newspaper is good; to watch your offspring play sports is even better.

So sports have mattered to me—maybe more than they should have. But, in considering this lifelong addiction to athletics, I need to offer some kind of rationale for it. What do we gain from sports, and what do sports teach us? Is a lifelong addiction to sports a colossal waste of time? Or is it a way to learn some hard truths that we humans all need to learn?

At the risk of becoming far more philosophical than reality warrants, let me tick off some ways sports can help us, some reasons sports matter:

Sports help us get in physical shape. I can't tell you how many weights I've lifted, miles I've run, sit-ups I've endured, or other exercises I've performed in my life, but the number must be staggering.

When I was playing sports in my younger years, I worked hard to stay fit and be game-ready. Now that I'm well past my sports prime and relegated to watching sports instead of playing them, I still work out three times a week at the gym and walk three miles every day.

Sports teach us the necessity of staying in shape. We can't be competitive in sports—or life—if we don't take care of our bodies.

Sports teach us discipline. The people who succeed in sports are the ones who discipline themselves and work at their craft. Not surprisingly, the people who succeed in life are the ones who discipline themselves and work at their craft, too. Sports remind us of the importance of both discipline and effort—two traits that translate well into any area of life.

Sports teach us how to be part of a team. Team sports teach us a host of life lessons about teamwork. We learn that we depend on others for our success, that we have to work in harmony to succeed, that we don't always get our way, that some people are more gifted at certain skills than we are, and that we need to encourage others if we want to succeed. Is there any endeavor in life that is not enhanced by a genuine spirit of teamwork? And for that reason alone, aren't sports a necessary and helpful life tool?

Sports teach us the law of sowing and reaping. If we don't put in the effort and training, we won't succeed in sports. Oh, there might be a few gifted superstars who can loaf along and do well, but most of us will reap what we sow. If we haven't run the miles, put in the practice time, lifted the weights, or heeded the coach's advice, we will not succeed. In sports, we nearly always get precisely what we deserve.

Sports teach us to take correction. Nearly all sports come with a grumpy, demanding coach who wants us to do things we don't want to do. We really don't want to run that extra mile, swim that extra lap, or play another nine holes.

But that irascible, no-nonsense coach is demanding it of us, so we bite the bullet and do it anyway. And, as we get older and no one is around to coach us, we might still have the discipline to correct ourselves and demand the best of ourselves. Sports teach us the necessity of accepting correction—either from that grumpy coach or from that little inner voice in our own heads.

Sports teach us how to fail. No one goes through life undefeated. As good and skilled as we think we might be, we eventually run into someone who is better. All four of my grandsons have played baseball, and I have probably given all of them my "baseball-is-a-game-of-failure" speech. Part of the profound truth I impart to them is that if they succeed only one time out of three as a hitter, they will hit .333 and be a whopping success. In other words, baseball is a game where you fail most of the time.

Anyone who plays sports eventually strikes out, fumbles, misses the free throw, drops the baton, or fails in some other way. No one who plays sports goes long without having to deal with defeat. Since life in general is that way, too, playing sports is good training for living life.

Sports give us reason to cheer. The good news is that sometimes we don't lose. Sometimes our team wins the championship, or we kick the game-winning goal, hit the game-winning home run, or score the game-winning touchdown. And even when we grow too old to play those games anymore, we still get to cheer because our team just won the big game or our grandson just got the game-winning hit.

I'm writing these words during the awful coronavirus pandemic and am finding that sports have become for me a bright light in a dark time. Hunkered down in our house, seldom seeing our kids and grandkids, and afraid to go to our favorite restaurants, Sherry and I are enduring, like the rest of the world, some long days.

But then the NBA started playing "under the bubble," and baseball teams started playing to empty stadiums. And those games gave us something to cheer about and look forward to. This dark pandemic time has made many of us realize how important sports are to us. Without sports to watch and teams to root for, some of us lost a big source of our delight. We all need reasons to cheer, and for those of us afflicted with this particular bug, sports give us reasons galore.

In 1989, I ran the one and only marathon of my life. My lifelong friend Steve Lee and I decided to run the Woodlands Marathon in Houston, and our wives and kids showed up to cheer us on. I had been training for months and had put in countless miles running through the streets of our neighborhood. But I had never run a marathon before and wasn't sure I was ready.

I have fond memories now of the race, but I also remember that running that race wasn't particularly fun. It was a warm, muggy day—not ideal for a marathon. I had set a goal of running the marathon in four hours or less and was on pace to do that until we got to mile twenty.

At that point, I "hit the wall." I was so tired and hot that my body decided to rebel. "I'm not going any further," it clearly said to me. "I quit having fun several miles back, and so this is as far as I'm going." I told Steve I needed to walk for a while, so we did. But then he said we could do it, that we weren't far from the finish line, that we hadn't come this far to quit now, so let's jog it in. Then we caught the faint strains of the theme song from *Rocky*, which was being played at the finish line.

If the finish line was that close, I told myself, maybe I could make it. Buoyed by Steve's encouragement and the *Rocky* song, I started to jog. As we approached the finish line, I even had a little kick and finished the race in 3:59:56. I had made my goal by four seconds. If I had had the strength, I would have raised my hands in victory.

That was my one and only marathon, and when I look back on it now I have nothing but fond memories. That marathon took place over thirty years ago, but as I reflect on it these many years later, I recognize most of the points I've just ticked off for you:

• *That marathon had forced me to get in shape.* I had put in countless miles preparing for it—and at about mile twenty wished I had put in a few more! But getting ready to run twenty-six miles had motivated me to be in the best shape of my life.

• *I had disciplined myself for months and followed a strict training schedule religiously.* Even on days I didn't feel like running, I had laced up my Saucony running shoes and hit the road.

• *I got to relearn the value of teamwork.* Marathoning is not exactly a team sport, but the smartest thing I did in my one-and-only marathon was to ask my good friend to run with me. He coaxed me to the finish line, and without his help I would not be telling you about this race. We were a team of two, and I desperately needed my teammate.

• *I got a reminder about the truth of sowing and reaping.* I got to the finish line because I had worked hard. I hit the wall at mile twenty because maybe I hadn't worked hard enough. The law of sowing and reaping is always in play in marathons, and runners nearly always wish they had sown a few more seeds—or, in this case, run a few more miles.

• *I was reminded of the importance of gentle correction.* In his own way, Steve was my coach that fateful day, telling me I could do more than I thought I could, encouraging me to keep going, prodding me to the finish line.

• *In reality, I failed.* I lost the race. Though I have been speaking of my performance in glowing terms, the real truth is that I finished way, way back in the pack. Hundreds (thousands?) of people crossed the finish line in front of me. I'm sure there were some children and gray-haired grandmothers who beat me to the finish line. But this time I didn't feel like a failure. Unlike those times I had struck out with the bases loaded or fumbled at the goal line, I crossed the marathon finish line with a great sense of satisfaction.

• *I got to celebrate in grand style.* Sherry, Stacy, and Randel gave me hugs and high fives at the finish line. People at church the next day congratulated me as if I had just won an Olympic medal. And, just in case a few parishioners hadn't heard about my triumphant run, I managed to work it into the sermon that day. I felt a real sense of accomplishment. I had finished the race. I had gotten under my four-hour goal. And, though I was sore all over, I had survived.

As I said, that was my one-and-only marathon. I'm not exactly sure why. Maybe it's because I learned how grueling a marathon really is. Maybe it's because I made my four-hour goal and never felt the need to try again. Maybe it's because I started having knee problems. Or, heaven forbid, maybe it's because I got too old. But, for whatever reason, that one race was the beginning and end of my marathon career.

It's revealing, though, that I'm still remembering that marathon and even telling you about it. I don't think it's the marathon itself that makes it so memorable to me. Had I won the race and carried home a hefty check and impressive trophy, maybe I would remember it for those things. But I got nothing from the race . . . but a limp and some severely sore muscles!

I think the reason I remember that race thirty years after it happened is connected to the good baggage that goes with it, the seven things I've mentioned that make sports so significant to many of us. We don't celebrate sports only when we win; we celebrate sports because of all the things we learn even, or especially, when we lose.

Chapter 4

Fascination Matters
Chasing Something that Gives You Delight

> *When I first started dating my husband, I had this weird*
> *fascination with the circus and old carnival things and*
> *sideshow freaks and all that. About a month after we*
> *started dating, he bought me this black-and-white photo*
> *book on the circus in the 1930s, and I started sobbing.*
> —Christina Hendricks

My lifelong fascination with sports is not the only fascination I've had. When I look back on my life, I see a long line of interests: model airplanes, baseball cards, coins, stamps, African violets, bonsai plants, books, vegetable gardening, writing, running, coffee mugs from colleges, and probably several more that I'm forgetting.

Throughout my life, I've discovered various and sundry things that have fascinated me and given me delight. Some of those fascinations lasted a few years and faded away; others have delighted me for a lifetime. I've come to believe that finding things that delight us—or, maybe better said, being found by things that delight us—keeps us from committing one of the seven deadly sins.

In the fourth century, a band of monks known as the Desert Fathers escaped to the wilderness in an attempt to live holy lives. While there, they compiled a list of the seven deadly sins that humans should avoid at all costs: pride, greed, lust, envy, gluttony, wrath, and sloth.

The sin that fascination saves us from is the last one on that list—sloth. The most obvious symptom of sloth is a repeated shrug of the shoulders. When we succumb to sloth, nothing matters much. Cars go unwashed, beds unmade, gardens untended, books unread, children undisciplined, and love unexpressed. When sloth does its dastardly damage to our souls, life becomes a meaningless treadmill. When sloth gets in its advanced stages, we don't see the wonder in even life's finest treasures. Sunsets bring no awe. Good music stirs no heartstrings. Speckled puppies evoke no chuckles. And little babies leave us cold.

The medical examiner would never officially declare it, but when a person gets to that point, they are unofficially dead—killed by the silent but deadly disease of sloth. Sadly, the world is full of dead people who are still walking, talking, and pretending to be alive.

This is where fascination comes to our rescue. When we find those things that delight us, when we start caring about those things on my list or yours, we keep sloth at bay. If we start caring now—about birds, mountain climbing, marathon running, crocheting, painting, or whatever catches our fancy—we will never succumb to sloth. We'll come to the end of our days still alive and brimming with life.

In his book *Bed and Board*, Robert Capon wrote,

> The tinfoil collectors and the fancy ribbon savers may be absurd, but they're not crazy. They are the ones who still retain the capacity for wonder that is the root of caring. When a little boy finds an old electric motor on a junk heap, he is pierced to the heart by the weight, the windings, and the silent turning of it. When he gets home, his mother tells him to throw it out. Most likely he will cry. It is his first and truest reaction to the affluent society. He usually forgets it, but we shouldn't. He is sane; society isn't. He possesses because he *cares*. We don't.[1]

There was a time in Jesus' ministry when he brought a little child to him and used that child as an object lesson. He told the people in the crowd that they all needed to become like that little child. He said that they would never enter the kingdom of God unless they became like that child.

---

1. Robert Capon, *Bed and Board* (New York: Simon & Schuster, 1965), 116.

Jesus didn't spell out all the implications of that statement, which leaves us wondering exactly what it was about that child that we should emulate. Several possibilities come to mind. Perhaps he was suggesting that adults need to have the *trust* that children have. Children are by nature trusting of adults and assume that adults will treat them fairly. So too, maybe Jesus was saying, we adults need to trust God and assume God has our best interests at heart.

Or perhaps Jesus was implying that adults need to have the *humility* that children have. Children know that they don't know, that they are little people who must depend on big people. So too, we adults need to quit pretending that we know it all, readily admit our ignorance, and trust the sovereignty of God.

But it is also possible that Jesus was implying that adults need to have the *wonder* that children have. Children are, by nature, endlessly fascinated by things that adults take for granted. A baby is enthralled by Grandma's glasses. A toddler can't keep her hands off the kitten. We adults learned a long time ago that there's nothing special about a pair of glasses and that kittens are a dime a dozen. But don't try to convince a little child of that. No little child is afflicted with sloth. But give that baby time, let them grow up to be a jaded adult, and they might just become one of the walking dead.

Whatever Jesus was implying that day when he told the adults in his crowd to be like the child in his lap, we all know from experience that children tend to have more wonder than we do. Children are full of fascination. Us? Not so much. Over the years, sloth seeps into our souls, and our wonder fades.

That's why spotting an adult who still has wonder is such an encouraging thing. I watched one night a human-interest story on the ten o'clock news about an older man who loves steam engine trains. This man has had a longtime love affair with these old trains and even bought one of his own some years ago. Occasionally he fires it up and chugs through his town, waving at wide-eyed children startled at the sight of an antique train huffing and puffing down their street. When the man spoke to the interviewer about steam engine trains, his whole being radiated excitement.

That television piece didn't tell *why* the man was so in love with trains. Perhaps he had ridden in a steam engine train as a boy and had fond memories of it. Perhaps his father had been the engineer on a steam engine train. Perhaps he had come from a long line of people who loved those trains. But the reason really doesn't matter. What matters is that he had found a special fascination that animated and delighted him.

And just watching that piece on the ten o'clock news animated and delighted *me*. My spirits rose considerably, and I later wondered why. Why would a brief TV piece about a man who loves steam engine trains so lift my spirits? The answer to that question, I realized as I thought about it later, is that delight always breeds delight. Fascination produces fascination. And wonder, almost without fail, is contagious.

So let's hear it for all the people around us from whom we can catch joy. The farmer meticulously plowing his field. The housewife lovingly baking her cinnamon rolls. The woman in the nursing home hand-stitching her pillowcases. The little boy enthralled by the old electric motor he found on the junk heap. The carpenter hand-crafting her cabinets. And last, but certainly not least, the old guy tooling around town in his train. All of these people have one thing in common: they have not succumbed to sloth, and their fascinations will probably assure that they never will.

I will try to notice these people every chance I get because they remind me of a crucial truth: sloth is both common and deadly in our world, and we should do everything in our power to avoid it. Fascination *matters* because it keeps sloth at bay and literally keeps us alive.

Chapter 5

Writing Matters
Surviving a Blissful Affliction

If you want to be a writer, there are two things you must do above all others—read a lot and write a lot.
—Stephen King

For at least the last fifty years of my life, I've been fascinated by writing. Several years ago, I even wrote a book titled *Blissful Affliction: The Ministry and Misery of Writing*. I began the book with this story:

> Nearly forty years ago, I boarded an airplane and flew to Minneapolis, Minnesota, to attend the Billy Graham School of Christian Writing. Looking back on it now, I'm surprised I went. I was a penniless seminary student, newly married, and had only flown a couple of times in my life. It seems foolhardy and bold now to think I would head off by myself to Minnesota to attend a writers' conference. But I did it, and I now think of that brave trip as the beginning point in a long quest to learn to write.
>
> The only thing I remember about the conference is that someone broke into my room at the YMCA where I was staying and stole all of my cash. I had to get Sherry, my wife, to wire me money so I could survive in Minnesota. If I learned any new writing techniques at that conference, I certainly don't remember them. But I did come home from the trip convinced that I wanted to write. It solidified what I suspected: writing was in my blood.[1]

For better or worse, richer or poorer, writing *has* been in my blood these past fifty years, and I have spent countless hours hurling

---

1. Judson Edwards, *Blissful Affliction* (Macon, GA: Smyth & Helwys, 2011), 1.

words at paper (or screens). I've written a number of books, hundreds of Bible studies for *Formations Commentary*, and countless newspaper and magazine articles. Looking back on the ponderous pile of stuff I've written, it's pretty obvious that I've written far more than I know.

And those are just the things that have been published. I've also written drawers full of brilliant stuff that has never found its way into print. A children's novel. A mystery novel. An insightful book on the Sermon on the Mount. Scores of articles. Early on, I even wrote verses for greeting cards that the greeting card people evidently didn't find inspiring.

But for fifty years, I've been fascinated by writing and hoping to make a small difference in the world through the written word. I titled that book *Blissful Affliction* because that is what writing has been for me. I think both of the words in that title need to be explored to get an accurate picture of the writing life.

Let's start with the second word first. Writing is an *affliction*, something that haunts and stalks a writer. E. B. White, who wrote *Charlotte's Web* and several books of brilliant essays, once observed, "Writing is not an occupation, nor is it a profession . . . . It is more of an affliction, or just punishment. It is something that raises up on you, as a welt."[2] That has been my experience, too, and I can think of a couple of obvious reasons why writing qualifies as a major affliction.

For one thing, writing doesn't usually pay the bills. Many people think of writers as living a glamorous and luxurious life. They've read of certain best-selling authors who have made millions of dollars and assume that writing makes people rich and famous. I am living proof that this is a myth. Though I have no statistics to verify this, I would guess that 99 percent of all writers make their living doing something else. They write because they're afflicted by it; they do something else because they have to eat.

When my first book, *A Matter of Choice*, was published in 1983, I was filled with the thrill of it all. I suddenly had to mull over a number of exciting options. Should I consider becoming a full-time writer? Should we start looking for a lake house we might

---

2. E. B. White, *One Man's Meat* (New York: Harper & Row, 1938), 254.

want to buy? Should I clear my calendar for all the book signings and speaking engagements that would shortly be coming my way? Should I buy some new clothes for the television appearances that would be inevitable?

It was a heady time. Every Sunday, I checked the *New York Times* bestseller list to see if *A Matter of Choice* had made it. Every Sunday, I was surprised and disappointed to discover it had not. But I knew that happy, prosperous times were just around the bend. After all, I had a book published! In my mind, that meant fame and fortune were coming; they were just a bit tardy for me.

That fantasy came crashing down, though, with the arrival of my first royalty check. I opened that envelope with trembling hands and was amazed at what I saw. The figure on that check was incredible—but for all the wrong reasons. Could the publisher have made a mistake? Misplaced a period? Forgotten a few zeros? Sent me the check intended for a lesser writer? I don't remember exactly how much that first royalty check was for; I do remember that our family of four blew nearly the whole thing on a meal of Whoppers at Burger King.

That first royalty check was a cruel lesson about the glamour of writing, a lesson that has been verified in many other royalty checks since. I learned that most of us who write will never become rich doing it. As I said, we don't write for money; we write because we're afflicted.

Not only is writing an almost impossible way to make a living; it is also an affliction because it is guaranteed to fill a writer's life with one frustration after another. Someone purportedly once asked Oscar Wilde if he had done any writing that day. He said he had added a comma to a sentence in the morning and taken it out in the afternoon. Every writer has experienced that kind of day. Some days, the words just don't flow. We write a while, read over what we have written, decide it's not good, and delete it. For every word that makes it onto the page, many more never see the light of day. Back in the days when I was typing on a typewriter and putting words on paper, I could fill up a trash can in short order. Writing a compelling, coherent sentence turns out to be harder than it seems.

But even when we have good days and the words come easily and quickly, our minds are filled with doubts. It's possible that this book or article will never be published, we tell ourselves. And even if it *is* published, few people will ever read it. And even if they do read it, they probably won't like it. The biggest enemy all writers face is discouragement. Some days going to the computer to work on a book or article is like going to a medicine cabinet to take a dose of castor oil. We don't do it because we *want* to; we do it because we *ought* to.

In his book *The Second Tree from the Corner*, E. B. White put it like this:

> The thought of writing hangs over our mind like an ugly cloud, making us apprehensive and depressed, as before a summer storm, so that we begin the day by subsiding after breakfast, or by going away, often to seedy and inconclusive destinations: the nearest zoo, or a branch post office to buy a few stamped envelopes. Our professional life has been a long, shameless exercise in avoidance. Our home is designed for maximum interruption, our office is the place where we never are . . . . Yet the record is there. Not even lying down and closing the blinds stops us from writing; not even our family, and our preoccupations with same, stops us. We have never counted the words, but we estimated them once and the estimate is staggering.[3]

Those of us who write know exactly what he is talking about.

So the question is, why even bother? Why bother to go to the computer to endure such affliction? If writing is so unprofitable and frustrating, why would any sane person do it? There seems to be some sort of literary masochism in the whole process, so why put yourself through that? Why not just turn off the computer and take up golf, cross-stitching, or something else that is enjoyable and even fun? Why not just say with Huck Finn, "There ain't nothing more to write about, and I am rotten glad of it, because if I'd a known how

---

3. E. B. White, *The Second Tree from the Corner* (New York: Harper & Row, 1935), 154.

much trouble it was to make a book I wouldn't a tackled it, and ain't agoing to no more," and give up writing once and for all?[4]

Well, because writing is not only an affliction; it is a *blissful* affliction. Sherwood Wirt, one-time editor of *Decision* magazine, wrote years ago, "Give me food and sleep and exercise, and put me in a room by myself with an electric typewriter, a Bible, some dictionaries, a synonym finder, and an idea, and for three hours I wouldn't trade places with anyone."[5]

Substitute the word "computer" for "electric typewriter," and those words could be mine. Some days, things just click—the ideas crackle, the words flow, and there's magic in the room. On those days, I lose all track of time, caught up in the joy of the writing moment. A few hours later I'll return to my senses, but for those magical hours I've been somewhere else, in a kingdom not inhabited by humans. "Caught up in the Spirit" seems to be as good a way as any to describe the experience.

And writing does pay some wonderful dividends—as I said, not necessarily *financial* dividends, but dividends nevertheless. Occasionally, someone will send a note or email thanking me for something I've written. Or someone will quote me in a book or article. Or someone will write a nice review. And, for that moment, I sense that maybe I've connected with another human being. All of us are trolling for kindred spirits, and when something I've written connects with a person, I sense perhaps that this miracle has happened.

We're all looking for companionship, for people we understand and who understand us. And the written word can sometimes make that happen. Once again, hear E. B. White:

> Why else would you be reading this fragmentary page—you with the book on your lap? You're not out to learn anything, certainly. You just want the healing action of some chance corroboration, the soporific of spirit laid against spirit. Even if you read only to

---

4. Mark Twain, *The Adventures of Huckleberry Finn* (New York: Penguin Classics, 2003), 400.

5. Quoted in William Gentz and Lee Roddy, *Writing to Inspire* (Cincinnati: F&W Publishing, 1988), 32.

crab about everything I say, your letter of complaint is a dead give-away; you are unutterably lonely or you wouldn't have taken the trouble to write it.[6]

I think he's right. We pick up a book hoping for chance corroboration, spirit laid against spirit. And most of us *are* unutterably lonely, looking for people who seem to know who we are and can provide us companionship as we journey through life.

Every time a writer writes something that connects with another person, that eases that person's loneliness, that lets that person know someone "gets it," a minor miracle has occurred. And that makes sitting at a computer for hours, wrestling with one word after another, well worth the effort.

I had decided several years ago that I had written my last book. I would continue to write the *Formations Commentary* and perhaps a few articles now and then. But no more books. I just had the sense that I had "run out of soap" and didn't have any more to say—at least not anything I hadn't said before.

But then this book idea knocked on my door. And here I am sitting at the study in my home flailing away at the computer again. Every afternoon, I sit here at my desk reflecting on my life and trying to write about what has really mattered.

When the book is published, I will not be checking the *New York Times* to see if it is on the bestseller list. I quit doing that many books ago. But if it connects with a few kindred spirits or brings a word of joy or hope to a few readers, I will have my reward. That's what makes writing a *blissful* affliction.

---

6. White, *One Man's Meat*, 79.

Chapter 6

Books Matter
Sitting at the Feet of Wisdom and Joy

A room without books is like a body without a soul.
—Marcus Tullius Cicero

I suspect my long fascination with writing can be traced back to an early fascination I had for reading. I remember clearly two series of books I read when I was maybe ten years old—the Bronc Burnett series and the Chip Hilton series. Wilfred McCormick wrote the Bronc Burnett series, which followed the exploits of a high school sports star in Sonora, New Mexico. Clair Bee wrote the Chip Hilton series, which, in like fashion, followed Chip and his friends through football, basketball, and baseball seasons at Valley Falls High School.

Each of those series had more than twenty books in them, which gave me fun adventures to read for a long time. I didn't read every book in those two series, but I read a lot of them. I would crawl into bed at night and quickly enter into a different world. Bronc was pitching in the state championship game for Sonora. Chip was throwing touchdown passes as the quarterback for Valley Falls High. And I was right there with them—and dreaming of the day when I, too, would be pitching on a state championship team or throwing touchdown passes.

Those sports books—and other books I read as a child—gave me hours of enjoyment and another world I could escape to if the real world ever got a little too heavy. I came to believe that books were wonderful things. And, somewhere in my young mind, there might have been a seed planted that made me want to write a book myself someday. Maybe I could become a Wilfred McCormick or Clair Bee and give someone else something to look forward to.

So early in life I became a bookaholic—an addiction that has
lasted a lifetime. On my days off when I was a pastor, my favorite
thing to do was browse in a bookstore. I could spend hours mean-
dering around Bookstop, Barnes & Noble, or some mom-and-pop
bookstore in our area. I wasn't just looking at books but smelling
them, feeling them, caressing them. Now that bookstores have
become an endangered species in our virtual culture, I spend hours
perusing books on my Kindle. It's not quite the same as holding a
real book in a real bookstore, but it's still a joy.

If I had to justify this lifelong infatuation with books, my justifi-
cation would go something like this:

*Every book is a visible expression of somebody's "insides," a portrait of
a personality.* Every book is an act of courage by the writer, an open
declaration of who that writer is and how that writer sees the world.
When we open a book, we get to peek into someone's soul.

Every book has a style and perspective all its own. Because no two
writers are alike, no two books say the same thing or express truth
in the same way. Books broaden us because they introduce us to so
many different people and viewpoints.

Every book offers us the opportunity for learning. Through books
we have access to the finest minds and spirits in history. I've never
met most of the authors I love, but I've learned from them all.

Every book grants freedom. Books give us total liberty to move at
our own pace, to agree or disagree, to continue reading or put them
back on the shelf. Unlike speeches, conversations, sales pitches, and
other forms of direct communication, books give us distance and
respect our privacy.

*Every book is an invitation to silence, a beckoning to flee the noise of
the world.* When I would crawl into bed as a boy with the adventures
of Bronc Burnett or Chip Hilton, I would heave a big sigh of satisfaction. Until I drifted off to sleep, I would be engulfed by silence
and the exploits of my fictional heroes. No worries. No expectations.
No noise. And though my reading choices are different now, I still
drift off to sleep most nights after silently escaping to another world
for a while.

Every book can be saved and treasured, referred back to, marked up, read to a friend, or passed along to someone else. Several years ago, I stumbled upon an old Chip Hilton book in a used bookstore and bought it for old time's sake. After all these years, Chip is alive and well in the pages of that old book written sixty years ago. And, I hope, he is still bringing joy to some little boy as he drifts off to sleep. Books last.

Every book is a concert of skillful people—writer, editor, artist, printer, binder, marketer, reader—all singing the same tune. Every writer eventually comes to appreciate what a community effort a book is. Though the book bears the author's name, he or she knows that the book exists because a team of skillful people has made it happen.

Every book has the potential to escort us into a better world. Books can cause sagging spirits to soar, make grieving souls smile, teach wayward minds the truth, or stir sluggish lives to action. When we open a book, we get the opportunity to sit at the feet of both wisdom and joy.

In light of all the remarkable things books do for us and in us, the question is not "Why are some people bookaholics?" but rather "Why aren't *more* people bookaholics?"

I'm not sure who I would be today if not for the Christian writings of Robert Capon, Frederick Buechner, Eugene Peterson, Karl Olsson, Barbara Brown Taylor, Henri Nouwen, Fred Craddock, and countless others who have tutored me in the art of Christian discipleship.

I can't think of much better entertainment than reading the mysteries of William Tapply, Sue Grafton, Philip Craig, Charles Finch, Will Thomas, and Louise Penny.

I can't think of a better way to drift off to sleep at night than reading the delightful novels of James Street, Joe Coomer, Jon Hassler, Wendell Berry, or Anne Tyler.

I can't fully delineate all the truths I learned about writing from John Jerome, Madeleine L'Engle, Bruce Lockerbie, James Kilpatrick, and E. B. White.

My long and enjoyable foray into the world of running was inspired and encouraged by the works of James Fixx, Joe Henderson, and George Sheehan.

If I add to that list the essays of Rick Bass, E. B. White, and Wendell Berry, I've still just begun to recall all of the writers who have given me hours of enjoyment and tons of insight through the years. I'm in debt to all of them for the wisdom and joy they've imparted to me in their books.

One of the most agonizing times of my life occurred when I decided to retire after thirty-eight years as a pastor. My agony came not from the decision to retire but from the realization that I wouldn't be able to keep all of my books in retirement. Over the years, I had accumulated well over a thousand books. I never had a problem finding shelf space for those books because the churches I served had ample bookshelves. I lined my study walls at the church with bookshelves and stuffed those bookshelves with books. But when I decided to retire, three ugly truths descended upon me.

First, I would never read or need many of the books I had accumulated. I still had old seminary textbooks, novels I had read many years ago, and countless books I knew I would never look at again. Was it really wise to keep those old books when I retired?

Second, I didn't really want to have to move those books. The thought of having to put those books in dozens of boxes and load them into a truck didn't sound enticing.

Third, I realized I didn't have room at home for all of my books. There was plenty of room in the study at church, but trying to squeeze them into my study at home wouldn't be easy. And buying all the bookshelves to accommodate those books wouldn't be cheap.

So the solution was obvious—but painful. I needed to get rid of most of my books. It seemed almost heretical even to think about it. Those books had been on my shelves for years and years. They were old friends who had taught, entertained, and inspired me. It seemed cruel and unthinkable to load them into boxes and send them away. Who in his right mind just banishes his friends?

But I knew it was the right thing to do, so I did it. I started taking a few boxes at a time to Half-Price Books and was embarrassed for my printed friends to discover just how valued (or devalued) they were by the secular world. Theological tomes filled with scholarly wisdom brought fifty cents. Old novels that had given me hours of joy went for almost nothing. Those old and faithful friends who had been with me forever were worthless to the rest of the world. Taking those books to Half-Price Books was an embarrassing, disheartening experience.

Some of my most treasured books made the cut, though, and claimed a proud place on a much smaller bookshelf in our home. I'm still buying books and adding to my pared-down collection. And I'm still ordering books for my Kindle and reading them daily. I suspect that I will go to my grave buying and reading books because I have learned from years of experience that books *matter*.

Chapter 7

Laughter Matters
Finding Levity in a Heavy World

We cannot really love anybody with whom we never laugh. —Agnes Repplier

As I mentioned earlier, I'm writing this book during the coronavirus pandemic that has invaded our world. These are dark, depressing, and dismal days. There was a time, not long ago, when I worked out three mornings a week at Anytime Fitness. Ate beef fajitas every Thursday evening at Jardin Corona. Rooted for our grandsons at their baseball tournaments. Saw our kids and grandkids on a regular basis. Attended church on Sunday mornings. And wrote at Starbucks every afternoon. But not anymore.

Now I spend most days marooned in the house. Sherry and I still take a three-mile walk every morning, but the rest of the day we spend hours at home—reading books, watching sports on TV, taking naps, and trying our best not to die from boredom. The highlight of many days is our rousing game of Skip-Bo before bed. The days all seem the same, and we often ask each other what day of the week it is.

A couple of weeks ago, my sister Laurie called from her home in Houston to check on us. We talked about our families and did some "catching up," and then she started telling me a funny story about a woman in her Sunday school class. This woman had a hilarious experience while trying to share her faith with someone on a city bus. The more Laurie told me this woman's story, the more tickled both of us became. Eventually we were both in tears, completely out of control.

When we hung up, two thoughts hit me. First, I realized how seldom I've laughed lately. The pandemic is part of that, I'm sure.

But I also think I've grown more serious and somber as I've gotten older. I remember getting tickled like that frequently when I was younger. I used to lose control on a regular basis and laughed until I cried frequently—and sometimes in embarrassing places like a church choir loft. That conversation with Laurie made me want to "lose it" a little more often.

The other thing that hit me is how good it felt to laugh like that. When I hung up the phone, I felt more refreshed and hopeful than I had felt in a long time. That laughter proved to be therapeutic. And it made me remember a quote I had highlighted in a book I read many years ago. I went to my bookshelf and was happy to see that the book had made the cut and was still in my collection.

The book is titled *The Earth Is Enough*, by Harry Middleton. It's his true story of growing up on a hardscrabble farm in the Ozarks with two old men, Albert and Emerson. In the portion I highlighted, Albert starts telling a story and eventually is overcome with laughter: "He was laughing now, his bony chest shaking so that you could almost hear his rib cage rubbing against his skin." Then Middleton writes,

> Emerson caught the laughter, then me. How I loved the sound of their laughter, how good it was just to laugh and laugh until you hurt, how the laughter took some of the pain out of the hard moments, the ones that hacked away at you day in and day out, impervious to resolution, to any remedy except that sound of the three of us laughing, laughing until we cried.[1]

That's why laughter matters. Because it takes the pain out of the hard moments. Because it bonds you with the people who are laughing with you. And because there is a growing school of thought that laughter literally unleashes healing forces in our bodies. Proverbs 17:22 declares, "A cheerful heart is good medicine, but a downcast spirit dries up the bones." Much in modern medicine seems to verify the truth of that verse.

---

1. Harry Middleton, *The Earth Is Enough* (New York: Simon & Schuster, 1989), 182.

Years ago, Norman Cousins wrote a bestselling book titled *Anatomy of an Illness*. Cousins had been diagnosed with a serious disease that had a most serious-sounding name—*ankylosing spondylitis*. He had read Hans Selye's book *The Stress of Life*, which detailed the negative effects of negative emotions on body chemistry. Cousins assumed that the opposite reality might also be true:

> The inevitable question arose in my mind: what about the positive emotions? If negative emotions produce negative chemical changes in the body, wouldn't the positive emotions produce positive chemical changes? Is it possible that love, hope, faith, laughter, confidence, and the will to live have therapeutic value?[2]

Cousins decided to test that hypothesis and embarked on a most unusual treatment. He shunned ordinary medicine and opted for big doses of vitamins and regular times of laughter. Every day he had a projector brought into his room and watched funny movies. A surprising thing happened: he made remarkable progress! Tests were run "before laughter" and "after laughter," and they always showed a marked improvement after his gleeful sessions at the movies.

I used to have two people I could rely on to make me laugh. I suppose they were my version of those funny movies. One was Don Knotts on the old *Andy Griffith Show*. He played the role of Deputy Barney Fife, right-hand man to Sheriff Andy Taylor, played by Andy Griffith.

Barney was full of bluster and bravado, but it was a false bravado. He was frail, fragile, and fallible, but he didn't want anyone to know it. Skinny, fearful Barney Fife trying to convince the people of Mayberry that he was tough and ferocious made him a most lovable and hilarious character. You had to love him and laugh at him at the same time.

I still remember a particular episode because I used it in a sermon one Sunday. In this episode, Andy tells Barney that they need to investigate a haunted house in Mayberry. Barney initially acts like he's eager to take on the haunted spirits in that house. But the more

---

2. Norman Cousins, *Anatomy of an Illness* (New York: Norton, 2005), 12.

he thinks about it, the more fearful he becomes. Finally, he realizes that he's too afraid to go to that haunted house and reluctantly confesses his fear to Andy.

Andy, keenly aware of who Barney really is and always understanding, tries to bolster his deputy's spirits. "Just remember, Barn," Andy says, "all you have to fear is fear itself." To which Barney replies, "But Andy, that's exactly the problem. What I have is fear itself!"

Some pastors quote Brueggemann, Tillich, and Bonhoeffer. After I saw that show, I quoted Barney Fife. I used that episode to remind our church that sometimes we have fear itself, and when we do, it's not a laughing matter. Barney's funny quip that engendered a lot of laughs when he said it on TV also enabled us to face a painful truth: life is sometimes a fearsome thing, and we all have to deal at times with fear itself.

But blustering, insecure Barney Fife was always one of my favorite characters and a surefire source of laughs when I needed them. He still brings a smile when I have to face fear itself and would just as soon not.

The other character who would always make me laugh was Tim Conway on *The Carol Burnett Show*. He was a part of a comedy cast that included Carol Burnett, Vicki Lawrence, and Harvey Korman. The show always involved several skits that they would perform together, and they were consistently funny.

But the funniest skits were the ones where Tim Conway would veer off script and start improvising. He was a comic genius and could ad-lib things that were absolutely hilarious. Even funnier, though, were the reactions of the cast when Tim would take off on one of his crazy tangents. They would try their best not to laugh, but they couldn't hold back. Harvey Korman, especially, would "lose it" when Tim started ad-libbing. The cameraman would inevitably zero in on Harvey Korman, knowing that his unsuccessful attempt to stifle his laughter was just as hilarious as Conway's antics.

When I read that Tim Conway died, I went on YouTube and watched some old clips of *The Carol Burnett Show*. I was happy to see that they're still as funny as ever. Tim doing his crazy shenanigans. Harvey and the rest of the cast doing their best to hold it together.

And, I'm quite sure, everyone watching them getting a hearty and much needed laugh.

It is both interesting and revealing to realize that human cultures have always had some version of Don Knotts and Tim Conway. As far back as 425 BC, a comedy writer named Aristophanes was writing funny plays, eleven of which survive and are still being performed. Even ancient cultures had clowns and jesters to bring humor to people. And people in those cultures, as in ours today, were willing to pay them to make audiences laugh.

Why are we humans willing to do that? Why do we pay people to make us laugh? Why do we go to movies that make us laugh? Why do we watch funny sitcoms on television? And why is it that every culture has funny men and women who are paid handsomely just to make people laugh?

Perhaps it's because we sense, even in ways we can't fully articulate, that laughter matters. Maybe it just makes us feel better. Maybe it makes us healthier. Maybe it helps us forget, at least for a brief moment, the heavy burdens in our lives. Whatever the reasons, we know we need to laugh. And we know we'll go to great measures to make that happen.

I'm not quite ready to toss away my medication and resort only to funny movies, but I do believe that positive emotions heal us. There's no doubt in my mind that a cheerful heart really is good medicine. In his book *The 2000-Mile Turtle*, H. B. Fox wrote, "Next to love, laughter is the best answer to the universe."[3]

Laughter *matters*. Laughter heals. Even—or especially—when you're marooned in your house during a pandemic, and the highlight of your day is a bedtime game of Skip-Bo.

---

3. H. B. Fox, *The 2000-Mile Turtle* (Austin: Madrona Press, 1975), 115.

Chapter 8

Scripture Matters
Wrestling with the Word

The Holy Scriptures are our letters from home.
—Augustine

In Genesis 32, Jacob has a mysterious wrestling match with an unknown assailant. Everything about that wrestling match is strange. The assailant is unnamed and unidentified. Jacob insists that he will not let the man go until the man blesses him. Jacob's hip is dislocated during the tussle. The man changes Jacob's name to Israel. Jacob realizes that this bizarre struggle is with God. And Jacob, or Israel, limps away from the encounter at daybreak, his life forever changed. There is nothing normal about anything in that story.

But when I read that strange story in Genesis, I think about my own wrestling match with the Bible. I mentioned earlier that I tried to read the Bible every day even when I was a young boy. Those early encounters with Scripture were the beginning of what I now see as a lifelong wrestling match with the Bible. I've been reading the Bible, teaching the Bible, preaching the Bible, writing about the Bible, and trying to live the Bible my whole life.

Like Jacob, I've often whispered to Scripture, "I will not let you go until you bless me." Like Jacob, I've found that this wrestling match has changed who I am and how I see myself. Like Jacob, I know that this wrestling match is, in truth, a struggle with God. Like Jacob, I've been wounded and confused by my encounters with Scripture. And like Jacob, I've limped away from many Bible studies forever changed.

But when I look back on my lifetime wrestling match with the Bible, I realize how much I still *don't* know about it. When it comes to

Scripture, my ignorance far outweighs my understanding. I'm living proof that a person can spend a lifetime studying the Bible and still not come close to exhausting its truths. The Bible still intimidates me, humbles me, and teaches me. But, after a lifetime of struggling with the word, I can tell you a few things about the Bible that I can affirm and celebrate with confidence.

First, Scripture gives us a new way to see the world. One of the things the Bible does for us is open our eyes to a new world, a world we might not even notice if the Bible didn't call it to our attention. Neurological experts tell us that our brains are equipped with a reticular activating system, which serves as a filter to let some things in and keep some things out. There is so much stimuli around us that we can't possibly take it all in, so our reticular activating system decides what we see and what we don't see.

That explains why we can open a desk drawer every day and not see the screwdriver that has been there forever, or why we can look out at a crowd and fail to notice Mary, who is sitting in the front row. The screwdriver and Mary are there in plain view, but they get filtered out by our reticular activating system.

As Jesus reminded people frequently, that same phenomenon can happen spiritually. We humans can look out at life and never once see God. God is there but goes unnoticed. As Jesus put it in the Sermon on the Mount, we can become so fixated on what we eat, drink, wear, and possess that we don't even notice God. Like that screwdriver in the drawer and Mary on the front row, God is there, but we don't have "eyes to see."

And that's how the Bible comes to our rescue. It reminds us that God *is* there and not to be ignored. It tells us not to neglect the spiritual dimension of life. It gives us a new way to look at the world. It invites us to look at it through God-colored glasses. Once we put these glasses on and wear them for a while, we do start to see the world from a different perspective. We learn of God, Jesus, prayer, forgiveness, grace, and righteousness. We discover a cross and an empty tomb. We learn about Peter, Paul, and the woman at the well. The Bible introduces us to a whole dimension of life and a whole array of characters we wouldn't see without it. As we immerse ourselves in this Scripture world, we start to change. Old things pass away, and all things become new.

I'm reminded of a short story by Nathaniel Hawthorne called "The Great Stone Face." It's the story of a young boy who is so entranced by a face carved in stone that he stares at it for hours on end, day after day. After months of being transfixed, the boy's face eventually is transformed into the image of the stone face he has looked at for so long. That's what Scripture can do for us and why we need to stare at it as often as we can.

Second, Scripture changes and develops over time. There's no telling how many well-intentioned folks have decided that they need to become better acquainted with the Bible. They have heard from others that reading the Bible can be a life-changing experience, so they decide to read it for themselves. They begin at the beginning, with the creation story, Adam and Eve, Noah and the ark, and the other people and events described in Genesis. Then they move on to Exodus, Leviticus, Numbers, and Deuteronomy, and my guess is that they lose their fervor about there. By the time they get to the end of the Pentateuch, they've become convinced that maybe the Bible isn't really the inspiring book it's cracked up to be.

They thought they would discover how to have a better family, how to handle their emotions, how to find the joyful life they crave, or some other crucial component of abundant life. Instead, they stepped into a strange and ancient world that seemed to have nothing in common with the one in which they live. They encountered bizarre dietary laws and precise instructions on how to sacrifice animals to God. They encountered a God who seems to talk out loud. They even encountered a God who commanded the Israelites to slaughter their enemies. All of this is foreign to their world and their personal experience. In frustration, they quietly put the Bible aside, secretly wondering how it could be so meaningful to other people.

My advice to those people would be to start over again, only this time start with Matthew. The Bible is a book that develops and progresses over time. Its thought changes and develops as the centuries go by. If we ever doubt this, all we need to do is reread the

Sermon on the Mount where Jesus takes six Old Testament laws and
either updates them or changes them altogether. He uses the formula
"You have heard it said of old . . . but I say to you . . . ," and then he
proceeds to bring the old laws up to date.

That passage in Matthew 5 underscores the fact that Scripture
moves and changes—which is why we need to be careful about pulling
out some obscure passage in the Old Testament and demanding that
people believe it "because it's in the Bible." If we desired, we could
use the Bible to justify war, slavery, racism, polygamy, the denigration
of women, and the stoning of disobedient children. People *have* used
the Bible to rationalize some of those things. But the passages that
prescribe those things aren't Scripture's final word on those subjects.
Scripture *moves*. And we need to move with it.

Third, Scripture is a rambling love letter. Just think of this one
fact: the Bible was written over a period of 1,400 years. When we
remember that the United States of America is less than 250 years
old, we realize how long it took for the Bible to be written. It was
written over all of those centuries by kings, shepherds, fishermen,
physicians, tentmakers, preachers, and prophets. It contains poems,
allegories, short stories, proverbs, prophecies, Gospels, letters, and
apocalypses. The Bible I'm using has almost 2,000 pages. No wonder
we sometimes feel overmatched when we try to understand it. And
no wonder few of us ever feel as if we've exhausted the Bible's riches.

So what's the point of it all? If the Bible is really that long and
complicated, how can we ever hope to get down to its essence? Well,
that depends on who you happen to ask. People read and interpret
the Bible in all different ways—as is evidenced by the thousands
of sects and denominations that call the Bible their handbook. We
Christians have one book but thousands (millions?) of interpreta-
tions of that book.

For me, though, the Bible is a rambling love letter. It winds and
bends all over the place, often confusing us in the process. But there
is a subtle storyline if only we have the eyes to see it. All of those
strange laws in the Pentateuch, all of those scathing prophecies by
the prophets, all of those heartfelt psalms by the psalmists, all of
those gospel stories by Matthew, Mark, Luke, and John, all of those

letters from the pen of the apostle Paul, and even that mind-blowing apocalypse at the end of the book all point to this truth: God loves us. That's the bottom line of Scripture.

And that truth leads me to my final thought about Scripture: *Scripture introduces us to the Living Word.* The final, ultimate word of Scripture is not a written word but a living Word: Jesus of Nazareth. But you don't have to take my word for that. Listen, instead, to the writer of the book of Hebrews:

> Long ago God spoke to our ancestors in many and various ways by the prophets, but in these last days he has spoken to us by a Son, whom he appointed heir of all things, through whom he also created the worlds. He is the reflection of God's glory and the exact imprint of God's very being, and he sustains all things by his powerful word. When he had made purification for sins, he sat down at the right hand of the majesty on high, having become as much superior to angels as the name he inherited is more excellent than theirs. (Heb 1:1-4)

The final, governing word in Scripture is Jesus, the Living Word, the reflection of God's glory and the exact imprint of God's very being. By the time we get to the end of the Bible, the one, overriding truth that stands out is the arrival of Jesus in history and his death and resurrection to reconcile all things to God.

If those frustrated people who gave up on the Bible back there in Leviticus will just keep reading, they will eventually get to the "good part." And they will realize why so many people refer to Scripture as good news. Those negative passages in parts of the Bible turn out not to be the final word in the Bible. The final, governing word is Jesus and his reconciling death on the cross for all people.

I'll give you one more illustration and then bring my "why the Bible matters" chapter to a close. Imagine the Bible as a circus, which, if you think about it, is a pretty accurate depiction. The Bible is full of action, color, and larger-than-life characters, much like the circus.

Like the circus, the Bible has a bunch of sideshows and a center ring. Circus sideshows might include the world's largest man, the world's strongest woman, and other assorted fascinating characters.

Scriptural sideshows could include Old Testament laws and customs, Paul's counsel to first-century churches, and John's wild visions in the book of Revelation.

But the center ring attraction in the Bible is Jesus. Ultimately, we end up at the foot of a cross and at the entrance of an empty tomb. We see a crucified and risen Lord who has given us the best picture of God we will ever have. And we realize that all of those words in Scripture, written by all of those people over a span of 1,400 years, have ultimately led us to him.

I'm happy to say that my wrestling match with the word is a tussle still in progress. For years, I studied the Bible every week as I prepared sermons to preach on Sunday. When I retired, sermon preparation was no longer required. But then I was asked to write the *Formations Commentary*, a guide for those who teach Bible study classes in churches. That means I still get to open Scripture and try to provide insight to others who teach Bible study classes in churches. I think I've learned more about the Bible as I write these commentary pieces than I did in all of my years at seminary.

Almost daily, I get out my Bible, open the commentaries, turn on my computer, and get ready to wrestle with the word. Like Jacob in Genesis 32, I usually whisper to the Bible in front of me, "I will not let you go unless you bless me." And, if I wrestle hard enough and persevere, the blessing nearly always comes.

Chapter 9

Music Matters
Listening to the Sounds of Life

Where words leave off, music begins. —Heinrich Heine

I learned to play the ukulele when I was eight years old. My cousin Jim Mullens also learned to play the ukulele about that time, and we formed a two-boy musical group we called "The Gold Dust Twins." I was the spokesman and introduced us by saying, "We're 'The Gold Dust Twins.' I'm the gold; he's the dust." That always brought the house down. Our career was brief, primarily because our grandmother had only so many women's groups that needed entertainment.

I didn't know it at the time, but "The Gold Dust Twins" were the beginning of a lifetime of music for me. I moved from the ukulele to the guitar to the five-string banjo. In high school, I played the banjo in a nine-person folk group called "The Spring Singers." That group won several talent shows in the Houston area and made us think we were on the way to becoming as famous as "The New Christy Minstrels."

In college, I played the guitar in a trio fashioned in the image of Peter, Paul, and Mary. Steve Lee, Brenda Rhame, and I traveled all over central Texas, singing primarily at banquets at Baptist churches. We never made much money, but we sure ate well.

When I became a pastor several years later, my guitar became a crucial part of my ministry. I accompanied children's and youth choirs, strummed it at midweek worship services, played it in a group of five guys known as "The Amigos," and even did an occasional sermon in song. When I look back on a long career as a pastor, I nearly always see myself with a guitar case in my hands. I was part minister and part minstrel.

So music was a vital ingredient in my ministry. But that just refers to the music I *played*; it doesn't include all of the music I listened to over the years. When I think of the albums, tapes, CDs, radio shows, concerts, choral anthems, hymns, and solos I've listened to, I've probably spent several years of my life just listening to music.

Even now, I begin every day with music. Sherry and I wake up early, sip coffee in bed while we read the paper, and listen to some of our favorite CDs on a small CD player in our bedroom. I don't think it's stretching the truth to say that music has been the backdrop for my whole life. Needless to say, music has mattered to me—and continues to matter to me. When I try to think of why that is, I'm reminded of some of the ways that music blesses our lives.

Music introduces us to fascinating people who will travel with us all of our days. As a teenager, I would often drift off to sleep at night listening to the smooth sounds of a folk trio known as "The Pozo Seco Singers." The group consisted of Susan Taylor, Lofton Kline, and Donnie Williams. They sang soft folk songs with a tight harmony, ideal for falling asleep to, and I listened to them almost every night. But they only put out a couple of albums, the group disbanded, and I lost track of them.

Several years later, I was driving alone in my car when I heard a song on the radio that caught my attention. A deep baritone voice was singing, "I'm just a country boy; money have I none; but I've got silver in the stars and gold in the morning sun, gold in the morning sun." At the end of the song, the deejay said, "That was Don Williams and his new single, 'Country Boy.'" It dawned on me that Donnie Williams of the Pozo Seco Singers had become Don Williams, country music vocalist.

I immediately bought the *Country Boy* album and would proceed to buy every album and CD Don Williams put out for the next forty years. It wasn't just the velvety voice and soothing music that got me; it was the shared history that Don and I had. I listened to him when I was a teenager, and I listened to him when I was sixty years old. He had become an important part of my personal history, though he never knew it. I went to several of his concerts, including one of the last he ever performed. He came to the Paramount Theatre in

Austin in late 2016, and the large crowd gathered there sang along with nearly every song.

Don Williams died on September 8, 2017, and a part of me died with him. But he is not the only singer I've bonded with over the years. I also felt my life was diminished when Perry Como, John Denver, Karen Carpenter, Glen Campbell, Eva Cassidy, Natalie Cole, and many others died. These were people who had been traveling with me for a long time, and they would be sorely missed.

Music does that for us. We find individuals and groups whose music speaks to us, and they bless us all of our lives. Every morning when I drink my coffee and read my paper, I slip another CD into the player and prepare to listen to some of my friends. I'm certain that some of these friends will travel with me the rest of my days.

Music creates and confirms community. There's something about music that brings people together. Music has a unique power to convey solidarity, sympathy, and a shared spirit. When we Americans gather for a significant event of some kind, we often stand together and sing our national anthem. When we do that, we immediately feel a kinship with all who are gathered there. Though we don't know one another, we all pledge our love and allegiance to our country. We might be strangers, but we're united in our love for America. And singing that song reminds us of that.

That's not the only time we sing to create and confirm community. We do it before the high school or college football game when we sing our school song. We do it when we join everyone in the baseball stadium during the seventh inning stretch and sing "Take Me Out to the Ballgame." We do it when we gather for weddings and funerals so that we can express our happiness or sadness together. We do it when someone turns a year older and we join together to sing "Happy Birthday." And we Christians do it every Sunday as we gather to worship, sing our songs of praise, and declare ourselves to be a *community* of faith.

Music is simply one of the best vehicles we have for declaring solidarity, affirming a shared allegiance, and fostering oneness with other people. What do we humans do when we want to join together to celebrate? We sing!

Music takes us where words can't go. The lyrics to songs are important, but they're not necessary. Bach and Chopin had no trouble composing enduring music that contained no words. We've all probably attended a symphony performance or piano concert that touched the deepest part of our being without a word ever being sung. That's the magic of music. It reaches down into the essence of who we are and stirs our emotions, with or without words.

If we're sad and need to have our spirits lifted, music will take us there. If we're sad and need music that quietly acknowledges our sadness, music will take us there too. If we know how and where to look, we can find music that will accompany us through the emotional seasons of life we have to traverse—loneliness, grief, ecstasy, fear, excitement, or wherever we happen to be emotionally or spiritually.

I've spent my life saying and writing words. I shudder to think how many words I've spoken from pulpits and written in books and commentaries. I would like to believe that at least some of those words "hit people where they lived" and made a difference in their lives. But I also know that words are limited. They tend to reach the head but not always the heart. Music, on the other hand, is aimed primarily at the heart. Music doesn't help us *learn* something; it helps us *feel* something.

There have been times in my life when I've gotten a lump in my throat because of something I've heard in a sermon or read in a book. Words matter because they help us learn. But I can't tell you how many times I've gotten a lump in my throat because of a quiet harmony, a breathtaking melody, or a virtuoso violin solo. When I have those experiences, I'm always reminded that music matters . . . because it helps us feel. It takes us where words can't go.

Music escorts us into the presence of God. When I was pastor of the Woodland Baptist Church in San Antonio, a large choir sat behind me every Sunday when I preached. Typically, the choir would sing a call to worship from the foyer, process into the sanctuary, sing an anthem before the sermon, and then sing a benediction at the end of the service. Occasionally, visitors in our worship service would tell me they came to Woodland because they had heard how good the music was. I don't remember one person telling me they came because they heard how good the preaching was.

I used to tell people that having such fine music in our services took a lot of pressure off of me as the preacher. I told them that even if the sermon on a particular Sunday fell flat, the music most certainly would not. Worshipers could still have a moving worship experience because the magnificent music would rescue the mediocre preaching. I would say it jokingly, but it wasn't a joke. I knew that music has the power to escort people into the presence of God.

When I retired and we moved to the Austin area, Sherry and I found ourselves in a most unusual situation. For the first time in forty years, we had to find and choose a church. For most of our lives, churches had found and chosen us. Though we never formally spelled them out, we had some definite requirements as we sought a church home. We wanted a church with biblical, insightful preaching. We wanted a church that shared our theological perspective. We wanted a church that ministered in specific, meaningful ways. And we wanted a church where we could meet people who could become our friends.

But perhaps at the top of our list was this one: we wanted a church that had quality, worshipful music. We knew that, for us, music was vital to our worship experience and that without good music we would have a hard time worshiping God. I'm fully aware that modern Christians define "good music" in different ways, but we needed music that would enable us to *feel* our faith and escort us into the presence of God. Having to find a church for the first time in forty years reminded both of us how crucial music is to our worship experience and our relationship to God.

If we should ever question how crucial music is to our lives, all we need to do is imagine a world *without* music.

Imagine a world without your favorite singing groups or solo artists.

Imagine a church service without hymns, anthems, the Doxology, or the tenor who always gives you chills.

Imagine a baseball game without "Take Me Out to the Ballgame" during the seventh-inning stretch or a football game with no band.

Imagine attending a wedding or funeral with no music to help you express your emotions.

Imagine Christmas with no carols.

Imagine, heaven forbid, drinking your coffee and reading the paper in the morning without your favorite musical friends to keep you company.

Let's just acknowledge how drab and flat our world would be without music. And then let's make it a priority to make as much music and listen to as much music as we possibly can.

Chapter 10

Faith Matters
Gambling on God

Faith is taking the first step even when you don't see the whole staircase. —Martin Luther King

Everyone has faith. It's impossible to live even one day without it. Every time we fill a prescription, take an airplane ride, face rush hour traffic, or just get out of bed in the morning, we're taking a leap of faith. Most of the time we don't even think of those as risky activities. They're just a normal part of life. And they are normal—because life is literally filled with risky propositions.

Sometimes we're aware that we're doing something that demands an extra measure of faith. When we join the military and go to battle or when we parachute out of an airplane, we're keenly cognizant of the risk involved in those activities. And when we decide to marry someone or to give birth to a child, we sense that we're taking a giant leap of faith as well. We know it's possible that neither the marriage nor the child will survive.

So faith is built into the fabric of human existence, and even the most irreligious among us have faith in spades. But the kind of faith I'm thinking about in this chapter is faith in God. As I've already mentioned, that kind of faith has shaped my whole life since I was baptized when I was seven. My faith in God has shaped my personality, my vocational choice, my relationships, my writing, my finances, and my emotional health. Take away my faith in God, and I'm a shell of myself.

I'm fully aware that my faith in God has been determined by a lot of factors. If I had been born in Pakistan to Muslim parents, I doubt seriously that I would have become a Baptist pastor in Texas.

We're all shaped by where, when, and to whom we are born. And I happened to be born in Corpus Christi, Texas in 1948 to Travis and Irene Edwards. My mother was Methodist, and my father was Baptist, but by the time I came along they had settled into the Baptist church.

I grew up in that culture—the Southern Baptist faith of the 1950s and '60s. I went to Sunday school, Vacation Bible School, Training Union, and Royal Ambassadors. I attended revivals and summer youth camps. I even went to church visitation each week to invite others to come to our church and, hopefully, find faith in God. I went to a Baptist university and seminary, worked at a Baptist children's home, and was pastor of three Baptist churches.

Looking back on it now, the faith I inherited was not perfect at all, but the pluses far outweighed the minuses. I learned about God, Jesus, the Holy Spirit, prayer, giving, witnessing, and other basics of faith. Though I have modified—and even dropped—some of the things I learned in those early years, I'm grateful for the faith I inherited.

But when we Christians speak of faith in God, what exactly are we talking about? It seems that the answer to that question varies from group to group, denomination to denomination. And when we turn to the Bible to try to get a firm definition of faith, we get verses like this: "Now faith is the assurance of things hoped for, the conviction of things not seen" (Heb 11:1).

Frankly, that verse doesn't help us much, does it? It does tell us, though, that faith involves *hoping* for something (or Someone) and trying to *see* something (or Someone). I preached many sermons on faith through the years and never felt like I came up with a slam-dunk definition of it.

I always had the feeling that faith is too big to try to capture in one definition. It's like that giant elephant the ant tried to describe. It was just too big to see from one angle, so the ant had to crawl all around it to realize just what an elephant was. In a sense, I've spent a long lifetime crawling around and observing faith in God. So, in the spirit of that ant, let me try to tell you what I've seen.

Faith is a gamble. By its nature, faith in God involves risk. Those who decide to have faith in God, in other words, are gamblers. They've looked at the evidence available to them and have decided to live as if God exists. But those who have decided *not* to have faith in God are gamblers as well. They've looked at the evidence available to them and have decided to live as if God *doesn't* exist. The bottom line is that when it comes to faith in God, we're all gamblers.

People like me who have decided to have faith in God can completely understand why some people might look at the evidence and decide not to take that leap of faith. There are many obstacles to a life of faith in God, and honesty demands that we acknowledge them:

- If there is a God, why doesn't He or She come out in the open? Why all of this silence and mystery?
- If there is a God, why do such bad things happen to such good people? Shouldn't God do something to keep people from suffering so much?
- If there is a God, why isn't the Bible more comprehensible and compelling? Shouldn't a book about God be clear and unambiguous?
- If there is a God, why do so many prayers go unanswered? Shouldn't God be responsive when we humans cry out in anguish and despair?
- If there is a God, why would that God allow all the different religions and sects in our world? Shouldn't God be more straightforward and plainspoken so that we humans could agree on divine truth?
- If there is a God, shouldn't God's followers be loving and gracious? Shouldn't God's people be above pettiness, dissension, and outright evil?
- If there is a God, why do I feel such an absence of God in my own life? Shouldn't God want to reveal Himself or Herself to me?

I could add more items to that list, but you get the idea. Those who have opted not to have faith in God have some compelling reasons for their decision. And those of us who have decided to have faith in God have to get over a number of significant hurdles to keep running the Christian race.

We Christians who have taken a leap of faith are bucking some compelling evidence against the existence of God. We're gamblers, and some would even say foolish gamblers, living under the spell of wishful thinking.

Faith is grateful. That's an imposing list I've just made for not having faith in God. If we left it at that, we might all quit going to church, stop reading the Bible, burn our ordination papers, and embark on a journey of atheism or agnosticism.

But that's just one side of the equation. While it's true that people of faith have many hurdles to clear on their journey through life, it's also true that there are many justifiable and compelling reasons for living a life of faith. Why do we Christians continue to live a life of faith? Let me count the ways.

- If there is no God, how do we account for the miracle of creation? Is the universe just a product of chance and happenstance? Or was there a Creator and Mastermind of the whole miraculous plan?
- If there is no God, how do we account for love? How do we explain how we feel about our children, our spouse, the wonder of life?
- If there is no God, how do we explain the faith of biblical people who lived and died trusting in a Divine Being who loved them and guided them through life? Were they just misguided? Is Scripture just a compilation of false information?
- If there is no God, how do we explain the faith of the people we love and trust the most? Were our parents, church friends, pastors, and other significant people in our lives mistaken? Or were they passing along to us the faith that had sustained them all of their days?
- If there is no God, how do we account for the way the Bible has transformed our lives? In spite of its eccentricities and difficulties, hasn't the Bible made our lives better?
- If there is no God, what do we do with Jesus? Has there ever been a more amazing and loving person in human history? And, if Jesus thought it crucial to have faith in God, shouldn't we take him seriously?

- If there is no God, how do we account for those moments when we sensed a divine presence in our lives? Were those moments merely chance and coincidence? Or were they legitimate encounters with God?
- If there is no God, whom do we have to thank for the wonder of our lives? When we look at the sunset, watch the ocean waves roar, sit around the fireplace with our family drinking hot chocolate, or realize how incredibly blessed we are, whom do we have to thank?

I remember a story I heard Fred Craddock tell years ago. He said he was talking to a young woman and asked her how she had become a Christian. She told him this story. She said that she tiptoed into the bedroom of her newborn baby one night and watched the baby gently sleeping in her bed. Incredibly, this child was hers, the product of her love for her husband, and she could scarcely take in the joy of it all. She said she was so overcome with wonder and gratitude for that child that tears filled her eyes. And then she told Craddock that's when she took her leap of faith. "I knew I had to have Someone to thank," she said.

I think that's the way faith happens for many of us. We're so grateful for creation, or love, or our family, or the Bible, or Jesus, or that baby sleeping in the crib that we have to have Someone to thank. Our faith is tied to gratitude. And, for some of us, that gratitude trumps all the reasons not to have faith in God.

Faith is dynamic. That is to say, faith changes and develops as we get older. Nearly thirty years ago, James Fowler wrote a book titled *Stages of Faith* in which he suggested that faith develops in a series of six predictable stages. Some people get stuck in one of the early stages of faith, Fowler says, and never go further. Some move all the way to stage six. Though the book is not an easy read, its primary point can be expressed in one simple sentence: faith is supposed to be dynamic. As we mature chronologically, we're supposed to mature spiritually.

In *The Truing of Christianity*, John Meagher describes his journey of faith like this:

Over the years, I have thought, and then dropped, approximately
thirty-seven editions of God, have cringed before some of them,
manipulated others, defied a few, ignored some, and in a few cases
tried to think about it as little as possible, for fear that God would
disappear if thought about much. And, indeed, approximately
thirty-six editions of God did disappear. I don't miss them. I now
feel persuaded that God will not disappear, whatever may happen
to my current and future editions, and I want to think about God
in a way that will not collapse under inspection, that can face up
to everything and stand in all weather.[1]

What this implies is that doubt is a crucial part of mature faith. In
the memorable words of Frederick Buechner, doubts function as the
ants in pants of faith. Our doubts push us to change, to drop some
inadequate editions of God so that we can find a better one. I'll have
more to say about this later in the book.

When it comes to fashioning a life of faith in God, these words
from the apostle Paul can serve as our marching orders: "Brothers
and sisters, do not be children in your thinking; rather be infants in
evil, but in thinking be adults" (1 Cor 14:20).

Faith is comprehensive. Faith is not just about a slice of our lives
we call "spiritual." In the eyes of the biblical writers, faith in God
affects every dimension of our lives. That must have been what the
apostle Paul had in mind when he reminded the Corinthian Christians that "if anyone is in Christ, there is a new creation: everything
old has passed away; see everything has become new!" (2 Cor 5:17).

The operative word in that verse is *everything. Everything* old
has passed away, and *everything* has become new. Those who are "in
Christ" have every nook and cranny of their lives affected by that
decision.

When we read Paul's two letters to the Christians in Corinth,
we notice that he addresses a multitude of issues—like food, sex,
marriage, and lawsuits. Those are not usually considered to be "spiritual" issues, but that was precisely the point Paul was trying to

---

1. John Meagher, *The Truing of Christianity* (New York: Doubleday, 1990),
7–8.

make. The Corinthians' commitment to Christ would affect even the "unspiritual" facets of their lives.

Perhaps the most obvious example of this truth is Jesus' Sermon on the Mount in Matthew 5–7. True, Jesus has some things to say about "spiritual" things like prayer, fasting, and giving alms. But most of the issues he addresses in that sermon are not necessarily religious. He speaks about happiness, influence, anger, adultery, divorce, speech, retaliation, loving enemies, money, worry, and self-deception. If we Christians take the Sermon on the Mount as our manifesto, it will constantly remind us that faith in God touches every dimension of our lives.

It's always tempting to equate faith with belief, as if faith in God is synonymous with believing the right things about God. Certainly the Christian faith is built on some theological beliefs, most notably beliefs about the life, death, and resurrection of Jesus of Nazareth. But those beliefs are to motivate us to change every facet of our lives. We believe . . . and because of that, we become a new person.

As Jesus puts it in the Sermon on the Mount, "Not everyone who says to me, 'Lord, Lord,' will enter the kingdom of heaven, but only the one who does the will of my Father in heaven" (Matt 7:21). Only the one who *does*. Only the one with a comprehensive faith. Only the one in whom *everything* has become new can claim true faith in God.

It has been a long time since I first expressed my faith in God and was baptized. My spiritual journey since that day has taken many twists and turns, but I find myself looking back on it with a great deal of joy.

Yes, I still sense the gamble at the heart of my faith. I may well be a religious fool, seduced by wishful thinking.

Yes, I continue to be filled with gratitude and surprised by the "wonder-full" things I see and experience. I still find plenty of reasons to be "faith-full."

Yes, I continue to doubt, change, and mature. I still have a lot to learn and some new editions of God to discover.

And, yes, I still struggle with making God the God of every facet of my life. I still find it easier to preach and write about faith than to live it.

But of this I am fairly certain: faith in God has mattered to me for over sixty years and will continue to matter to me until I die.

Chapter 11

Tenacity Matters
Taking One More Step

In the confrontation between the stream and the rock, the stream always wins—not through strength but by perseverance. —H. Jackson Brown

I was a pastor for thirty-eight years, which means that I had a lot of "got to" moments and a lot of "had to" moments. The "got to" moments were the ones that filled me with joy and delight, all of the wonderful things I *got* to do. The "had to" moments were the ones that were hard and filled me with dread, all of the difficult things I *had* to do.

What were some of the things I *got* to do as a pastor?

I got to preach the good news of Jesus Christ every Sunday.

I got to officiate at hundreds of weddings and celebrate with a happy bride and groom.

I got to hold many newborn babies in the hospital and share the joy with their ecstatic parents.

I got to eat at hundreds of dinners and banquets and feast on fried chicken, creamed corn, fruit salad, homemade rolls, and peach cobbler.

I got to attend ball games, recitals, concerts, and school events of church children and youth.

I got to strum the guitar at many church events.

I got to become friends with a host of fine, caring people.

The list could go on almost indefinitely. Suffice it to say, I got to do a bunch of enjoyable, rewarding things in my years as a pastor and occasionally felt guilty that the church would pay me to have such fun.

But that is just part of the story. I also had my share of things I *had* to do as a pastor.

I had to moderate quite a few contentious business meetings.

I had to attend hundreds of boring or heated committee meetings through the years.

I had to endure the agony of preaching a sermon that had so much promise . . . and fizzled on the launching pad.

I had to visit people in the hospital who knew they were dying and would never go home.

I had to deal with church conflict and watch as people I knew and loved left the church.

I had to stand at the graveside and try to comfort people who were justifiably beyond comforting.

I suppose that list could go on indefinitely as well, and when I was in the throes of some of those "had to" moments, it seemed only fair that I should be making at least as much money as LeBron James.

When I think back on those "had to" moments, though, the ones that still make me hurt are the ones where people experienced inexplicable, inconsolable losses. There were many times I felt that what people were experiencing was beyond words, beyond anything I could say or any Bible verse I could read. I could feel their pain but felt helpless to alleviate it.

One particular episode is still fresh in my memory. It was a Thursday when I was pastor of the Heritage Park Baptist Church near Houston. Thursday was my day off, a day I spent eating breakfast at Denny's with Sherry, browsing local bookstores, mowing the lawn, or playing tennis. But this particular Thursday, our church secretary called me at home to tell me a family had called the church and wanted me to come immediately to their house. I did that but was not at all prepared for what I discovered when I got there.

I was greeted at the door by a distraught couple, members of our church. They had returned home that morning to discover that their middle-school son had committed suicide. They found him in the garage with the car motor still running. He had done poorly on his report card, had been admonished by his parents to do better, and they assumed the matter had been sufficiently addressed. They had no idea he was so distraught, no idea he would even think of taking his own life.

What do you say to a fine, Christian couple whose fourteen-year-old son has just committed suicide? I don't remember now what I said. I probably stuttered some feeble words of comfort and said a prayer with them. Whatever I said or did, I'm pretty sure it wasn't particularly helpful. I was in way over my head there and knew it.

I preached Darren's funeral a few days later and remember how emotionally and physically drained I was when it was over. I remember trying to take my daily three-mile run through the neighborhood that night and having to walk most of it because I was so exhausted. If that experience did that to me, I thought to myself, what did it do to that boy's parents and older sister? I knew that they had just experienced something they would never truly get over, something that would change their lives forever.

How can anyone survive an experience like that? I think of many other people, too, in my thirty-eight-year ministry and ask the same question about them. A couple who lost a newborn baby. Spouses who lost a lifelong companion and best friend. Children who had abusive parents. How do people survive those things? As I said, whenever I encountered that kind of pain, I felt way overmatched. I was in the business of saying words . . . and words simply can't carry that much freight.

The best answer I can come up with for surviving that kind of pain can be summed up in one word: *tenacity*. People who survive those kinds of pain are tenacious. They decide that they will not quit. They will not stop living. They will not give up hope. Though they might not put it in these theological terms, they dare to believe that beyond their cross, there can be a resurrection.

I think I'm in pretty good company when I say that because the apostle Paul seems to have come to the same conclusion. Listen to him in Romans 5:3-5:

> And not only that, but we also boast in our sufferings, knowing that suffering produces endurance, and endurance produces character, and character produces hope, and hope does not disappoint

us, because God's love has been poured into our hearts through the Holy Spirit that has been given to us.

I'm guessing that Paul is giving us his own plan for surviving the awful hurts of life, and certainly he had more than his share of them. It's as if he builds a ladder from suffering to the love of God and shows us how to climb that ladder step by step.

The bottom rung is suffering, and we will all be on this rung at some point in our lives. Everyone has to suffer. Some suffer a little; some suffer a lot. But no one escapes this world without some hardship and trouble.

But notice the next rung on Paul's ladder: endurance, or what I'm calling tenacity. When suffering comes, the first attribute we have to summon is tenacity. We make a personal decision to take one more step, live one more day, pray one more prayer. We simply choose not to give up.

While summoning tenacity is by no means easy, it does clearly define our primary goal when some awful trouble invades our lives. What we have to do is endure, hang in there, not give up. We don't have to be happy and fake. We don't have to be a "good witness." We don't have to pretend we're not hurting. And we don't have to leapfrog to the top of the ladder in one fell swoop. We just have to endure.

When something catastrophic invades our lives, we're suddenly faced with some stark, mutually exclusive alternatives. We quit or we keep going. We despair or we find a ray of hope. We choose death or we choose life. And Paul says that if we will just endure, we will get to keep moving up the ladder.

Our tenacity, he says, will produce character. Circumstances won't necessarily change, but *we* will. The person who died will not come back to life, the tragedy will not be erased, and the pain will not magically disappear. But our character will change. Something inside of us will become different. Our suffering can certainly destroy us, but it can also make us a deeper, better, more loving person.

There will even come a day, Paul says, when a ray of hope will invade our dark world. After our character changes, we start to get hope. Though at times it's hard to believe it, there is coming a day when the sun peeks through the clouds. A day when we don't cry all day but even laugh a little bit. A day when God becomes a possibility again.

And at the top of Paul's ladder, that's where we end up: "hope does not disappoint us because God's love has been poured into our hearts." God returns to our experience. Faith flickers back to life. We start to think that God might still love us after all. But that doesn't happen overnight. We have to climb the ladder, one slow, painful step at a time.

The truth I've come to realize, though, is that the first, essential step in that climb is tenacity. Suffering has to produce endurance for the rest of the progression to unfold. If we don't endure, hang in there, persevere, the whole process breaks down. Tenacity *matters* because it is the key ingredient in surviving life's pain.

I don't remember now what passage of Scripture I used when I preached Darren's funeral those many years ago. I would guess, though, that I used my favorite verse in the Bible: "But those who wait for the LORD shall renew their strength, they shall mount up with wings like eagles, they shall run and not be weary, and they shall walk and not faint" (Isa 40:31).

That great verse addresses all the seasons we humans experience as we journey through life. At times, we get to mount up with wings like eagles. These are the times when we're flying high and life is perfect. We just got the promotion. Our child received the scholarship. Our marriage is happy and healthy. All is wonderful and well, and we're grateful to God for all of our blessings.

At times, we get to run and not be weary. These are the times when we're just moving through life, involved in a good routine, doing our work, loving our family, and finding plenty of strength to do whatever we need to do.

But then there are times when we have to walk and not faint. These are the hard moments in life—the times of loss, setback, depression, and almost despair. The task in these times is simply to walk and not faint, to practice the perseverance Paul wrote about in Romans 5.

Isaiah's promise is that we will be able to navigate all of these seasons of life if we will wait for the Lord. If we will tenaciously trust God, we will be able to celebrate the mountaintops, enjoy the routine of the daily race, and, maybe most crucially, survive the dark, lonely valleys. But, as in Romans 5, the key phrase is "wait for the Lord," which means being tenacious and never giving up.

I've lost track of those parents who lost their son that Thursday long ago. I stayed in touch with them for a long while, but then I moved to San Antonio and lost touch. The last I knew of them, they were still married, still loving their daughter, still working their jobs, and still believing in God.

I would like to think they survived that almost unbearable loss and made it all the way to the top of Paul's ladder. I would like to believe they kept waiting for the Lord, one long day at a time, until the sun started to shine again.

Chapter 12

Solitude Matters
Listening to Your Soul

> *I find it wholesome to be alone the greater part of the time. To be in company, even with the best, is soon wearisome and dissipating. I love to be alone. I never found the companion that was so companionable as solitude.* —Henry David Thoreau

There was a big oak tree behind my school, Ridgecrest Elementary. I can't tell you how many hours I spent in that big tree as a young boy, sometimes with friends and sometimes all by myself. It was close enough to our house that I could either walk or ride my bike to the tree, so I visited it several times a week. In a stunning display of precocious creativity, I even came up with a clever name for it: The Big Tree.

I still remember the feeling of freedom I had when I was sitting alone in The Big Tree. There was no noise, except for the rustle of the leaves. No people around to distract my thoughts. No pressure. No worries. No demands. Just the glorious freedom of solitude. Even as a third-grader, I didn't take that freedom for granted. And I wanted as much of it as I could get.

Frankly, I've never taken that freedom for granted and have spent a lifetime trying to get as much of it as possible. I've always found versions of The Big Tree as I've moved through the stages of life, ways to escape the noise and pressure of the world "out there." When I think about my life today, I still see Big Trees everywhere.

As I mentioned, I spend two hours every morning reading the paper and drinking a couple of mugs of coffee. It's dark outside, the cat sits on my lap, soft music plays in the background, and I get to study box scores, play word games, and read all the news I can stomach. So, in a way, I start every day in The Big Tree.

Then Sherry and I go on a three-mile walk. We have several beautiful trails near our house, and each morning we choose which one we will take. We stroll along in quiet conversation or blissful silence, counting our steps and our blessings all along the way.

In the afternoon, I usually spend a couple of hours writing—either in my study at the house or, pre-Covid-19, at a local coffee shop. It's just me, my laptop, a cup of coffee, and my thoughts. For those few hours I'm alone, enjoying all the benefits of The Big Tree.

At bedtime, I typically nestle in with a good book—no longer Bronc Burnett or Chip Hilton but whatever book I happen to be reading at the moment. I drift off to sleep after spending some quiet time with my latest novel or nonfiction choice.

What that schedule indicates, I think, is that I'm still having Big Tree moments, times I've intentionally carved out to save my sanity, to listen to my soul. Now that I think about my daily schedule in retirement, I may have taken up permanent residence in The Big Tree!

These times are important to me even in retirement, but they might have been more crucial when I was a "busy pastor." Forty years ago, I read Henri Nouwen's book *The Way of the Heart* and highlighted this passage about the temptations facing those of us in ministry:

> Just look for a moment at our daily routine. In general we are very busy people. We have many meetings to attend, many visits to make, many services to lead. Our calendars are filled with appointments, our days and weeks filled with engagements, and our years filled with plans and projects. There is seldom a period in which we do not know what to do, and we move through life in such a distracted way that we do not even take the time and rest to wonder if any of the things we think, say, or do are worth thinking, saying, or doing.[1]

---

1. Henri Nouwen, *The Way of the Heart* (New York: Ballantine Books, 1981), 10.

In addition to highlighting that passage, I wrote "Ouch!" beside it. I knew that this could be true for me, that I could become so busy being a "successful pastor" that I would lose my soul. So all through my years as a pastor I looked for Big Trees. I tried to find ways to be by myself, to stay in touch with my soul, to experience the blessed freedom of solitude.

For years, that included a daily run through the neighborhood. After a typical day of doing pastoral "stuff," like preparing a sermon, leading a staff meeting, visiting people in a nursing home, or planning Sunday's worship service, I would rush home, slip on my running shoes, and hit the road. For the next hour or so, it was just me, the wind, the road, and perhaps the smell of hamburgers cooking on someone's outdoor grill. It was a time to unwind, be quiet, think, and pray. A time to stop being a workaholic pastor and start being a free spirit.

During those running years, one of my gurus was Dr. George Sheehan. In his book *Running and Being*, he wrote,

> I like being alone. I enjoy my own company. I am satisfied running the roads far from any other human being. For me loneliness is the desirable state. Solitary confinement, a touch of heaven. . . . My mind works through association rather than logic or reason. When I run those miles over the roads there is all the while a stream of consciousness, a torrent of ideas, coursing through my brain. One idea after another goes hurtling past like so much white water. Giving me here and there a new insight, a new intuition, a new understanding. Each in turn soon replaced by yet another thought, still another idea.[2]

That was my experience, too, as I breezed through the neighborhood on my daily runs. I would get sermon ideas, discover insight on how to deal with a difficult person, think how great the breeze felt on my face, and feel myself unwinding. Like Sheehan, I liked being alone.

2. George Sheehan, *Running and Being* (New York: Warner Books, 1978), 222.

And I looked forward every day to my solitary romp through the neighborhood.

I'm keenly aware that not everyone needs solitude as much as I do. I once was asked to preach at a church in Virginia and was hosted by a pastor there whose needs were different from mine. When I got to the church, I realized that I would be preaching not just one Sunday morning service but three—a contemplative service, a traditional service, and a contemporary service.

I started the day in a clerical robe, preaching in the fellowship hall to a small group at the contemplative service. Then I hastily ditched the robe, put on a coat and tie, and sprinted to the sanctuary to lead the traditional service. Then I shed the coat and tie, put on more casual clothes, and preached to a younger crowd at the contemporary service.

By the time I finished that third service, I was exhausted. I felt like I had run a spiritual marathon and barely made it to the finish line. After that service, I was alone with the pastor in his study and told him how tiring that was for me.

"How do you do that every Sunday?" I asked him.

"Oh, I love it," he said. "Preaching three times every Sunday morning gets me excited and energized. I look forward to it every week."

I'm quite sure that he was telling the truth. He's an extrovert who thrives on people, activity, and excitement. He finds his joy in the crowd where the action is. I, on the other hand, am an introvert who thrives on being alone, having no agenda, and hearing the sound of silence. I tend to find my joy where the action *isn't*. Two pastors. Two temperaments. Two ways of coming at life. Neither is better or worse than the other. But both of us need to know who we are and focus on doing what keeps us alive, what feeds our souls.

Several years ago, Sherry and I flew to New England to watch our daughter, Stacy, participate in an Ironman Triathlon. While there, we decided to see some of the popular sights in that part of the world. We walked the Freedom Trail through downtown Boston, attended a Red Sox game, walked the campuses of Harvard and MIT, and sampled our first cannoli.

But one of my top priorities on that trip was to go to Concord and visit Walden Pond. I had been a Henry David Thoreau fan for a long time and wanted to experience Walden for myself. So we went. We walked all the way around Walden Pond. We saw where Thoreau lived and a replica of his cabin. We got to see up close where the supreme model of solitude and self-sufficiency "did his thing."

Perhaps Thoreau's most famous quote is this one: "If a man does not keep pace with his companions perhaps it is because he hears a different drummer. Let him step to the music which he hears, however measured or far away."[3] That was not just a quotable quote; it was a personal testimony. Thoreau was writing his own manifesto. He himself was hearing a different drummer. And, in going to Walden Pond, he was stepping to the music he was hearing, however measured or far away.

But the question is, how will we even hear that different drummer with so much noise all around us? And how will we step to the music we're supposed to be hearing if we never stop and listen?

Well, tragically, we won't. We'll go to our graves without ever knowing who we really are, what we really believe, and what we're really supposed to be doing. And that's why, I think, solitude *matters*. It helps us pay attention . . . so we can hear *our* drummer and step to *our* music.

---

3. Henry David Thoreau, *Walden* (New York: Signet Books, 2012), 84.

Chapter 13

Justice Matters
Seeing Everyone in the World as Your Neighbor

Justice will not be served until those who are unaffected are as outraged as those who are. —Benjamin Franklin

I grew up in a *Leave It to Beaver, Ozzie and Harriet* world. I watched those television shows every week because they were about "my people." The Cleavers and the Nelsons were White, middle-class, Protestant, heterosexual couples with families who were happy and well adjusted. When I watched those programs each week, I was looking in the mirror.

Frankly, it was a good world, and I sometimes still long for it. It was a simple world where everyone looked, acted, and believed the same. In my school and neighborhood, there were no people of color, no people in poverty, no people with a different sexual orientation, no people of a different religion, and no people who played odd games like soccer and lacrosse. We were all alike and all "normal," and we liked it that way.

We knew that there were people somewhere on the other side of the world who were not like us. We knew there were people of color out there and even saw some occasionally. We saw pictures of poor people on television. We heard there might be homosexuals in the world. We understood that there were pagan religions across the sea. And we knew that some countries played strange sports that made no sense to us.

But we also knew that we lived in the best world and that the rest of the world would give anything to be like us. We never saw ourselves as smug or condescending; we saw ourselves as blessed and thanked God regularly for our blessings. So we would watch Ward, June, Wally, and Beaver and be grateful that we were like them. And we would watch Ozzie, Harriet, David, and Ricky and identify completely with their middle-class bliss. Their world was our world, and it was a simple, happy world void of angst and turmoil.

Now fast-forward fifty or sixty years. The Cleavers and Nelsons are gone, not just because they grew old and died but because their world no longer exists. The world I'm living in now bears little resemblance to the world I knew back then. Now I see people of color everywhere. People from all over the world have come to Austin, and I see them in the grocery store, on the sports field, on the freeways, and in my grandsons' classes at school. Austin, like most cities, is a mosaic of people from all over the world. The Cleavers and the Nelsons are still among us, but they have a lot of company.

I also see poverty all around me. Homeless people set up tents on the side of our streets. People needing money carry signs at our traffic intersections. Our newspaper reminds us often that the food bank needs donations. It also tells us of immigrants stranded at the Texas border and families in our own city who are destitute. It is nearly impossible not to see the poverty at my doorstep.

I also see and hear from people whose sexual orientations are different from mine. They attend my church, go to my grandsons' schools, and live in my neighborhood. They know they are different from what society views as the norm, but they, like all people, yearn for and deserve acceptance.

I bump into different religious beliefs all the time now. Come to find out, not everyone in America is Christian. When Sherry and I drive to our daily hiking place, we pass three mosques along the way. The nearest Baptist church is several miles from our house; the nearest mosque is in walking distance.

And when we walk down to tend our community garden plot, we see kids playing soccer and lacrosse at our local park and a large group of Middle Eastern men playing cricket. Two of my own grandsons are the stars of their lacrosse teams.

Truly, I've lived long enough to say that I am now in a different world than the one into which I was born. As I said, there are days when I miss the old world, the world where everything was simple and homogeneous. This complicated, multicultured, multifaceted world is messy and not nearly as easy to traverse. But it's the world in which we find ourselves, and wise people adapt to it and see it as brimming with new possibilities.

When I look back on that old world now, I do so with both nostalgia and regret. Nostalgia because I had a happy, uncomplicated childhood for me. Like Wally, Beaver, David, and Ricky, I had a happy family, lived in a nice house, and enjoyed my life. If you happened to be White and semi-affluent, life was good back in the 1950s and '60s, and I got to experience and benefit from it.

The regret comes from being blind to the reality of those years. For much of my life, I wasn't intentionally prejudiced or calloused; I was unaware. Even in the old world, people of color, poverty, different sexual orientations, and different religious beliefs were there; I just never saw them. They never showed up on the radar of my experience. I was in a cultural cocoon and didn't know it. The final words in "Amazing Grace" have taken on a whole new meaning for me when I think back on those days: "was blind but now I see."

As far as I know, I have never been overtly cruel or prejudiced to anyone. I like to think of myself as a kind and compassionate person. My sin has not been one of *commission*, but of *omission*. I have lived too long in the *Leave It to Beaver* world and been slow to adjust to the realities that have now become starkly apparent.

What has become starkly apparent is that our culture is filled with walls that keep a lot of people cut off from respect, hope, and the basic necessities of life. They exist in a different world from mine, and, if I'm going to take Jesus seriously, I need to do my part in removing those walls. The word for this wall-removal project is *justice*, and it is the calling of every Christian.

Justice is at the heart of one of the most famous parables Jesus ever told. In his story of the good Samaritan, Jesus never once uses the word "justice," but that is what the parable is about. Every time we Christians read it, we are reminded of our marching orders.

Just to refresh your memory: A lawyer comes to Jesus asking what he needs to do to inherit eternal life. Jesus asks him what is written in the Law, and the man quotes the Great Commandment: "You shall love the Lord your God with all your heart, and with all your soul, and with all your strength, and with all your mind, and your neighbor as yourself" (Luke 10:27). Jesus tells him that his answer is correct. If he will live by the Great Commandment, he will find eternal life. But the lawyer probes further and asks who exactly is his neighbor. That gives Jesus the opportunity to tell him the story of the good Samaritan.

We shouldn't pass too quickly over the fact that Jesus uses a hated Samaritan as the hero of his story. He makes the respected priest and Levite the villains and the despised. That shocking fact may have offended this lawyer and any other respectable Jewish person who happened to hear the story.

As the story unfolds, the unlikely hero does three things—what I have now come to see as the three fundamentals of justice. First, he sees the wounded man on the side of the road. Second, he is moved to compassion. And third, he does something specific and tangible to help. *Seeing. Caring. Acting.* Those are the three ingredients of justice.

The *seeing* dimension of justice demands that we move beyond our comfortable, safe, and free existence to acknowledge that many in our world have none of those things. They're not comfortable. They're not safe. They're not free. And they likely never will be until people who do have those things reach across the divide to rescue them. It took me far too many years to see that my "*Leave It to Beaver*" world was not shared by everyone.

The *caring* dimension of justice means that we move beyond seeing to be bothered by the discrepancy we see. In Jesus' story, the priest and Levite also see the wounded man on the side of the road. But for reasons Jesus doesn't enumerate, they're not moved to help. They see the man, but they don't really care about his plight. They shrug their shoulders and hurry on to the committee meeting at the synagogue. The Samaritan, though, is "moved with pity," Jesus says. The motto of justice is, "What happens to you matters to me." The Samaritan shows us that clearly in this story. What has happened to the man lying on the side of the road matters to the Samaritan. The religious leaders see but don't care. The Samaritan sees and cares a lot.

The *acting* dimension of justice means that our caring compels us to do something specific and tangible to rectify an unfair situation. The Samaritan loads the man on his donkey, takes him to an inn, and binds his wounds. Then he tells the innkeeper to take care of the man and that he will repay him whatever he has to spend. Though Jesus doesn't say this in the parable, I would bet that the Samaritan showed up the next day . . . and the next day . . . and every day thereafter until the man was healthy and whole.

What this Samaritan is doing here is not headline material. It is quiet, personal, and mostly unnoticed. It is likely that only three people ever knew about this act of justice—the wounded man, the innkeeper, and the Samaritan himself. But justice is not primarily about making speeches, walking in marches, or being on social media, though those activities have their place. It is about seeing, caring, and acting in quiet, personal, mostly unnoticed ways to make a difference.

The person who practices justice has eyes to see the walls that line and divide our world. Those walls are everywhere, but not everyone sees them.

The person who practices justice is bothered by the presence of those walls, feels the unfairness those walls represent, and vows to remove them.

And the person who practices justice then does good Samaritan kinds of things. Takes in a wounded traveler. Helps build a house for a homeless person. Befriends the despised and friendless. Becomes part of a church committed to breaking down walls. Writes a check to the food bank. The list is endless, but the goal is always the same: to tear down walls and build bridges.

I still remember the day I got my first glasses. I was in the fourth grade and hadn't realized my vision was bad. But the optometrist said otherwise and prescribed glasses for me, and I went with my parents that day to try them on. I could scarcely believe what I saw when I looked out the window of the office. I could see individual leaves on the trees, definite features and expressions on people's faces, and clear numbers on license plates. I had been nearly blind and didn't know it.

I'm not sure what opened my spiritual eyes to my spiritual blindness. I was quite content in my *Leave It to Beaver* world and felt no need to ever leave it. It seemed to be a good and godly world, filled with good and godly people like me.

But one day I looked out at that world and saw walls. Economic walls. Racial walls. Sexual identity walls. Religious walls. In the church of my childhood, we used to sing an old hymn that went, "Whosoever will, whosoever will, shout the proclamation over vale and hill. 'Tis a loving Father calls the wanderer home. Whosoever will may come." But somewhere along the way, I saw clearly that this wasn't really true. We could sing the old hymn at the top of our lungs, but the truth was that only those like us could come. Only those from the *Leave It to Beaver* world would find a welcome among us. Others would find a series of walls carefully constructed to exclude them.

I'm not sure what opened my eyes to see those walls. Maybe it was just getting older. Maybe it was the private, painful discussions I had with hurting people in my church office. Maybe it was a few mission trips I took to South Texas. Maybe it was working closely with Hispanic people on our church staff. Maybe it was all of those experiences and many more.

But one day, I looked out the window and saw walls I had never seen before. And I knew that justice—and Jesus—wanted those walls removed.

Chapter 14

Doubt Matters
Finding a Better Faith

*Whether your faith is that there is a God or that there
is not a God, if you don't have any doubts you are either
kidding yourself or asleep.* —Frederick Buechner

In his book *Western Theology,* Wes Seeliger suggests that two
approaches to faith are prevalent in the Christian church: Settler
Faith and Pioneer Faith. Settler Faith is, well, settled. It is something
to be believed, protected, and held on to at all costs. Settler Christians live by the motto "God said it; I believe it; that settles it." There
is little room for questions and doubt. In Settler Faith, the church
is a fortress, designed to protect orthodoxy and keep the evil of the
world at bay.

Pioneer Faith, on the other hand, is still in process. It is an adven-
ture that takes a person on a wild ride of change and growth. Pioneer
Christians are constantly learning new truth and changing as they
travel through life. There is plenty of room for doubt because doubt
is seen as an invitation to find a better faith. In Pioneer Faith, the
church is a way station designed to offer instruction and encouragement to faithful travelers.

I grew up, I suppose, with a Settler Faith. One of the key compo-
nents in my faith development was a popular tract called "The Four
Spiritual Laws." The four laws were:

1. God loves you and has a wonderful plan for your life.
2. Man is sinful and separated from God. Therefore, he cannot
know and experience God's love and plan for his life.

3. Jesus Christ is God's only provision for man's sin. Through him you can know and experience God's love and plan for your life.

4. We must individually receive Jesus Christ as Savior and Lord. Then we can know and experience God's love and plan for our lives.

I was not only supposed to believe the Four Spiritual Laws but was also encouraged to get my friends and family members to embrace them. The Four Spiritual Laws were put on a tract to be mass-distributed to everyone I knew, and I often carried a few in my back pocket—though I usually lacked the courage to hand any to my friends.

There was nothing wrong or heretical about the message on that tract. But I had the distinct impression that once a person agreed to those four propositions, that was all that needed to happen in their life. They were "saved" and bound for heaven and could then try to get everyone else "saved" and bound for heaven, too. Once a person agreed to the four propositions on that tract, they had purchased a spiritual insurance policy that was good for eternity.

I also had the distinct impression that my life was going to be a long journey of trying to sell those insurance policies, of continuing to believe those four truths and convincing the people around me to believe them too. Frankly, it didn't sound like an exciting life. But if that was what God wanted me to do, I was willing to do it. As one schooled in Settler Faith, I had settled into a life of simple laws and a simple evangelistic assignment.

Somewhere along the way, though, I got a different view of what a life with God might involve. I began to see that it was more complicated, mysterious, and wonderful than those Four Spiritual Laws. And I also began to see that being God's representative in the world wasn't just passing out tracts to the people around me. It could be richer and more meaningful than that. I eventually became so intrigued by this new understanding of the Christian Way that I decided to pursue a life in vocational ministry, went to seminary, and spent thirty-eight years as a pastor.

What made that shift possible and inviting was the idea of finding and sharing with others a Pioneer Faith. Looking back on it now, I see that it all started with doubt. I started doubting my Settler Faith, with its tracts and simplistic evangelistic endeavors, and started wondering if the Christian experience was more challenging and intriguing than I had ever imagined. I started envisioning a journey with Christ as a journey of discovery, change, and growth. Maybe I wasn't supposed to believe and pass out tracts all my days; maybe I was supposed to become a new and better human being and invite others to join me on that road.

But, as I said, it was doubt that started the process. If you think about it, how will we ever find a new and better faith if we don't first doubt and question the old one? How can God possibly do something new and different in our lives if we never consider the possibility that this could happen? Doubt *matters* . . . because it is our ticket to a better faith and a better self.

We Christians should probably ask ourselves some questions from time to time to try to determine the condition of our current faith. These questions can help us take a spiritual inventory and perhaps be a catalyst in launching us on a life-enriching journey of doubt and change. I'm thinking of three questions that can move us from Settler Faith to Pioneer Faith.

The first one is, *Does my faith make me honest to, and about, God?* There's an old story about a little boy who went down front to be a part of the children's time at his church. As was the custom, the pastor circled the children around him and then asked them this question: "Can any of you tell me what has long ears, hops from place to place, and likes to eat carrots?" The little boy raised his hand, and when called on he said, "Well, it sounds like a rabbit to me. But the answer is probably Jesus again."

That little boy was smart enough, and had been in church enough, to know that there are certain stock answers that we Christians are supposed to give when asked certain questions. Just as there is a "political correctness" in our society, so too there is a "theological correctness" in our churches. Woe unto the person who dares to call a rabbit a rabbit. It's got to be Jesus again.

But that kind of parroted theology eventually loses its meaning. Faith has to be based on what we really think to be true, or it starts to become a charade. We become the "hypocrites" Jesus describes in the Gospels who wear a religious mask to hide who they truly are and what they truly believe. Any faith that doesn't connect to genuine conviction is a sham.

I suspect that there are many thoughtful people in the contemporary church who feel the pressure to believe some things they don't actually believe. They might even number themselves among the people Leslie Weatherhead once called "Christian agnostics":

> A Christian agnostic is a person who is immensely attracted by Christ and who seeks to show his spirit, to meet the challenges, hardships, and sorrows of life in the light of that spirit, but, who though he is sure of many Christian truths, feels that he cannot honestly and conscientiously "sign on the dotted line" that he believes certain theological ideas about which some branches of the church dogmatize; churches from which he feels excluded because he cannot "believe." His intellectual integrity makes him say about many things, "It may be so, I do not know."[1]

So what should these Christian agnostics do? Say they believe these things even if they don't? Pretend to believe so they can be accepted by the church? I think not. That would make them one of those hypocrites Jesus condemned. No, they should be honest, cling to the part of the biblical story they *can* affirm, and go from there. And the church should welcome them with open arms as honest seekers of the Truth.

Anytime we start saying we believe things that we don't really believe, we should start doubting our brand of faith. It's a faith built on the sand of theological correctness and religious peer pressure. I would be willing to bet that God is more pleased with an honest doubter than with a dishonest believer.

The second question is, *Does my faith give me joy?* No less an expert than Charlie Brown in "Peanuts" once said that joy is the most infallible proof of the presence of God. Charlie, I think, hit the nail

---

1. Leslie Weatherhead, *The Christian Agnostic* (Nashville: Abingdon Press, 1965), 15.

right on the head. The world will certainly know we are Christians by our love, but they will also know we are Christians by our joy.

I didn't know that for a long time. Back in the Settler days, I assumed that just the opposite was true. I assumed that God would inevitably call me to do something hard and demanding, something I really didn't want to do. I just knew I was bound for the jungles of Africa—primarily because I wanted so badly *not* to go there. I connected God to sacrifice, suffering, and obligation . . . never to joy.

But I always craved joy. I came to believe that maybe God did want me to be joyful, so I filled my library with books about joy: *The Key to Triumphant Living, Ask Me to Dance, Life More Abundant, Jesus Makes Me Laugh, That Elusive Thing Called Joy, Come to the Party, To a Dancing God*. In 1986, I quit reading books about joy long enough to write one myself: *Dancing to Zion*.

One writer who nearly always made me joyful was Robert Capon, who consistently celebrated the incredible grace of God in all of his books. In his book *Between Noon and Three*, he describes what happens when joy seeps out of our faith. He has his character Gertrude Schlosskaese say,

> When I look at my middle-aged children, I feel sad. It seems to me that instead of becoming freer as they've gotten older, they've gotten more and afraid of failure—to the point where they don't feel they can risk anything. And I wonder if that isn't due to the way they were raised—all the emphasis we put on being acceptable, all the fear of making mistakes we drummed into them. They're wonderful people, successful and responsible. But they're so depressingly conventional, so tight, so tense. . . . I was so afraid of their non-conformity when they were young, now it's their very conformity that frightens me. And the sad part is they don't even seem to be happy in their successes; they seem to be trapped by them.
>
> Grace really does have to be given more attention. If it isn't, all we'll see is grown people who are more afraid than children—and who have to hide from their fear in work, or drink, or a lot of other things that, as they use them, are just . . . well, joyless.[2]

---

2. Robert Capon, *Between Noon and Three* (New York: Harper & Row, 1986), 27.

That somehow rings painfully true. So many of us are wonderful people who are successful, responsible, and highly respected. But, truth to tell, we're also conventional, tight, tense, and . . . well, joyless. If we determine that this is true in our lives, it might be time to doubt our faith and take a big gulp of grace.

The third question is, *Does my faith make me kind?* Dare we plumb the depths of how *unkind* some brands of faith have been through the centuries? When we Christians look back at our history, certain facets of it make us shake our heads in embarrassment and shame.

People of faith crucified Jesus. People of faith launched the murderous Crusades. People of faith burned witches at Salem. People of faith bought, sold, and mistreated slaves. People of faith groomed and abused children in the church. People of faith became scandalously rich in the name of a penniless Galilean. I could go on, but that's enough. Just because a person claims to have faith doesn't mean that person is loving and kind. And just because a gathering of people claims to be a church doesn't guarantee that it is marked by love and grace.

Even if we're not guilty of such heinous acts, it might be wise from time to time to pause and ask ourselves if we're becoming kinder people. Are we becoming more irritable . . . or patient? Are we becoming more self-centered . . . or other-centered? Are we spending more money on self . . . or others? Does our faith prompt us to focus on doctrines and programs . . . or on people in need?

Passages like Jesus' parable of the sheep and goats in Matthew 25 remind us how simple our calling really is. In that parable, Jesus calls us to be kind. Feed a hungry person. Give a cup of water to someone who is thirsty. Welcome a stranger. Give clothes to someone who doesn't have any. Visit someone who is sick. Go see someone who is in prison. Those simple acts require no advanced degree in theology. They just require eyes that see needs, hearts that are moved to compassion, and hands that act in simple, tangible ways.

And, lest we forget, this kindness begins at home. It begins with our spouse, kids, grandkids, and anyone else who happens to reside at our house. It involves doing little acts of kindness that either make or break those relationships. In her book *Where the Wind Begins*, Paula D'Arcy reminds us,

> The formula for finding your primary mission is here: Put down this book. Walk outside your house, trailer, or apartment. Look in through a window. Now you see where Christ has sent you. Serving starts where you are. If you understand that your mission to the faces at your table, no matter how few, ranks in importance with a mission of a great evangelist to crowds of thousands, then you have begun to understand Love.[3]

Whenever we forget that, it's time to repent, to go back to the basics of Christian discipleship. And whenever we find ourselves critical, mean-spirited, and punitive, it's time to doubt our faith.

When we look at the list of awful acts committed by people of faith throughout history, don't we wish that, at some point in their lives, they would have doubted that faith? If only they had looked at their faith and asked the three questions I've just mentioned, thousands of lives might have been saved and the course of history might have looked very different. Christians with an honest, joyful, kind faith don't harm people; they bless them.

During my freshman year in college, I passed through a painful time of doubt. I didn't doubt the existence of God or any truth in Scripture; I doubted my own salvation. I started asking myself, "How could I, as a seven-year-old boy, possibly have made a serious commitment to Jesus Christ? Really now, how much can a seven-year-old boy understand?"

I convinced myself that my salvation experience wasn't real, that I hadn't understood what I was doing when I walked that aisle at the Westview Baptist Church and gave my heart to Jesus. I wrestled with the thought that I needed to do all of that over again now that I was a more mature nineteen-year-old. I needed to make sure that my salvation was secure—which probably meant walking the aisle and being

---

3. Paula D'Arcy, *Where the Wind Begins* (Carol Stream, IL: Harold Shaw, 1984), 95.

baptized again. I was miserable for weeks. I tossed and turned in bed at night, feeling like a spiritual impostor and trying to decide how to know for sure that I was a Christian. Doubting your salvation, I can tell you from experience, is not fun.

What finally rescued me from my agony was an article I happened to read by chance (or Providence?) in the Houston newspaper. It was written by Ruth Graham, the wife of Billy Graham, who had a regular question-answer column each week. The question that week concerned how and when she had become a Christian. I don't remember all of her answer, but to this day I still remember the line I needed to hear. She said she didn't remember the exact moment she had become a Christian, and then she wrote, "But just because you don't remember your birthday doesn't mean you weren't born."

That was music to my doubting ears. Maybe what happened when I was seven wasn't the crucial issue. What mattered wasn't what happened back then; what mattered was what was happening *now*. Did I have a relationship with God *now*? Did I want to live for God *now*? Ironically, even the fact that I was so concerned about my relationship with God bore convincing testimony that I had one.

I tell you that old story because it was my first brush with doubt. Up until that time, God had said it, I had believed it, and that had settled it. But my experience at the age of nineteen shook me and made me ponder my faith. Looking back on it now, I see that passing through my painful season of doubt was a step toward a better, more mature faith. I came to realize that a journey with God is just that: a journey. When or how you start is not the crucial question; the crucial question is, "Are you still moving?"

That, really, is why doubt *matters*. Our doubts are the ants in the pants of faith that keep us moving. They prod us toward a better faith. A faith that is honest to, and about, God. A faith that fills us with joy. And a faith that makes us kinder and more loving.

The great paradox of doubt is this: none of us want to doubt our faith, but none of us will ever have a better faith until we do.

Chapter 15

Creativity Matters
Feeding the Lake

> *You can't use up creativity. The more you use, the more you have.* —Maya Angelou

When our grandsons were small, they often came to our house to stay for several hours (or days) while their parents were away. We had a routine that we followed nearly every time they came. I would take them to Lowe's, Michael's, or Walmart, and we would find a "project" we could work on together.

Often it was a kit from Lowe's that they could hammer and glue to make a car, truck, bank, or some other small item. One time we bought a kit for a simple clock from Michael's. The all-time favorite was a rubber band gun from Walmart that they put together and then used to shoot down dominoes in the living room.

Not only did these projects give us something to do while the boys were in our care; they also gave them something to take home when they left. Something they could show their parents. Something they could put in their bedroom. Something that would be an insignia of their time at Mia's and Grandad's. And maybe, most importantly, something they had fashioned with their own hands.

Is there anything more gratifying in life than making something with our own hands? Creating something with our own imagination? Making something come into being because of our own initiative? Isn't that one reason we parents gaze at our newborn babies with such pride and wonder? Imagine: *we* created this miracle!

In the first chapter of Genesis, we read about the time God fashioned creation—sky, ocean, plants, trees, sun, moon, animals, and, finally, human beings. What is evident when we read that ancient story is how much delight God obviously took in creating those things. The recurring line in the creation story is "God saw that it was good." It's almost as if God would create something and have so much fun doing it that he just had to create something else.

Toward the end of the creation story in Genesis 1, the writer says, "So God created humankind in his own image, in the image of God he created them; male and female he created them" (Gen 1:27). For centuries, people have been quoting that verse and then speculating as to what it means. What does it mean that human beings have been created in the image of God?

Well, it could mean that human beings, like God, have the capacity to know good from evil and to make choices between right and wrong. Or it could mean that human beings, like God, have the capacity to give and receive love. Or it could mean that human beings, like God, have the responsibility of being stewards of the earth, of being sovereign over the other facets of creation.

But it is also possible that being made in the image of God means that humans, like God, have the capacity to create things, to bring new things into being. In light of the context, that might be the most obvious implication of this phrase. God has just had a delightful time spinning the whole world into existence, and then God saves the best for last. God fashions man and woman and then bestows on them the capacity to create—and to know the unmatched thrill that creating something new always brings.

Creativity belongs on my list of things that really matter because I have spent a lifetime trying to create things—sermons, songs, books, articles, friendships, a marriage, barbecue, and pecan pies, to mention just a few. Granted, many of those creations were failures, and probably no one would say I've ever produced greatness in any of my creations. But the desire to create has driven me and defined me even if my creations have sometimes flopped. This drive to create has blessed my life immeasurably. Let me try to count the ways that creativity enhances our lives.

Creativity provides us consistent joy. As I said, is there anything in life more gratifying than creating something with our own hands, minds, or talents? When we create anything worthwhile, it fills us with both pride and joy. We don't want to gloat about our handi-work, but secretly we look at the work of our hands or minds and say, "Wow, *I* created that!"

When my first book *A Matter of Choice* was published in 1983, I was filled with the pride and joy of creating a book. For all I knew at the time, it would be the one and only book I would ever write. So Sherry did a nice and thoughtful thing for me: she had the book framed so that I could hang it on the wall and remember it forever. On the more than likely chance that it would be my only book, I could relish it all my days.

But the joy of creating is addictive, so I tried to write another book. And, when it got published, we got it framed, too. That prac-tice became the tradition. Now, over many years of writing, the wall in my study has become lined with framed books—each with a history, each loaded with memories of its writing, each destined to make me happy when I see it hanging there. Almost no one sees those books but me. But no one else really needs to see them but me. After all, I created them, and I'm the only one who will get a rush of joy just seeing them hanging there.

I think that is true for creations of all kinds. Painting pictures makes artists joyful. Composing music makes composers joyful. Concocting innovative football plays makes coaches joyful. And cooking delicious meals makes chefs joyful. Any time we get to create something we love, joy is the inevitable serendipity.

Creativity enables us to express our uniqueness. What makes our creative endeavors special is their uniqueness. True, many authors have written books, many of them better written and more profound than mine. But still, none of them is exactly like mine. Just as no two people are ever duplicates, so, too, our creative endeavors are never duplicates either. Every time we create something, we are declaring who we are. Our creations have our unique fingerprints all over them.

Once upon a time, I was known for my pecan pies. I found a special recipe for pecan pies that I really liked, tweaked it a bit to make it even better, and started making them for our church staff every Christmas. For years, our staff members knew what I was giving them for Christmas because it was the same thing every year: a pecan pie.

I always gave those pies with pride, and the staff members were inevitably effusive in their praise: "Best pecan pie I've ever eaten." "Never had a pecan pie like this one." I have no way of knowing what they said to their spouse when they carried the pie home. They may have felt the freedom to say what they really thought: "I know he means well, but his pecan pies are not all that great."

But the reason I always gave those pecan pies with pride is because I had made them myself. They were the product of my own recipe and culinary efforts. Had I gone to the store and bought pecan pies, it just wouldn't have been the same. It was the uniqueness of those pies, the fact that they came from my own hand and oven, that made me proud to give them. Whatever we create—be it fine art, poetry, blankets, or pecan pies—we're making something unique, something we present to the world as a statement of who we are.

Creativity teaches us to fail. I'm making it sound like all of our creative endeavors are resounding successes. Our books always get published. Our pecan pies always get praised. Our art always inspires. Everything we create is always brilliant.

But, as good that sounds, it doesn't square with reality. The truth is, sometimes our creative efforts fail miserably. I've had some books published, but, as I mentioned earlier, I've had even more rejected. When I look back on some of those rejected manuscripts now, I breathe a sigh of relief that they weren't published. They seemed like literary masterpieces at the time, but now . . . not so much. Even some of the manuscripts that did become books sometimes make me grimace. Sometimes our creative endeavors are, in truth, not so creative, and as painful as it is to admit it, we have to live with that failure.

When I was in the seventh grade, I took wood shop because I thought it would be fun to make things out of wood and give hand-crafted gifts to my family. Our first project in the class was a small shelf in the shape of Texas. We had to cut a piece of wood to look like Texas, glue a shelf on it, sand it smooth, and shellac it to a fine sheen.

I found it to be a surprisingly frustrating experience. When I glanced around the shop, it seemed to me that my classmates' shelves looked better than mine. Their Texas was in the shape of Texas. Mine resembled Texas . . . but not much. I still remember how crestfallen I was when Mr. Bayh, our shop teacher, came by, inspected my Texas shelf, and said, "I think you have a lot of talents, Jud, but I'm not sure woodworking is one of them."

He was only telling me what I already knew. But it still hurt to have my fears verified. And his words have proven to be exactly right. I do have some talents, but woodworking is not one of them. That is the risk inherent in any attempt at creativity. The shelf might not look like Texas. The pie might be awful. The book might never get off the ground. The painting might look like something a first-grader would produce. So attempting to create is a dangerous risk. We come face to face with our limitations.

What our failures should do, I think, is make us keep looking for the things we *can* create. I can't make a Texas shelf, program a computer, fix anything mechanical, paint a picture, or crochet a rug. But I can cook a mean meal on the barbecue grill, strum the guitar and play the banjo, and write a mostly coherent sentence. I do have a few means at my disposal for creativity. And so, I'm sure, do you. Just because we can't create *everything* doesn't mean we can't create *something*.

Creativity enables us to make an offering to the world. Every creative endeavor can be seen as one person's attempt to serve others. The book, the pecan pie, the song, the computer program, the patchwork quilt—all are made to bless others. All are someone's expression of a servant spirit, someone's effort to serve the world.

If we think of the world as a giant lake, we each have a hand in feeding that lake and making it fresh and clean. It's truly a community effort, and each of us has to do our part. The writer Jean Rhys once wrote:

> Listen to me. All of writing is a huge lake. There are great rivers that feed the lake, like Tolstoy and Dostoevsky. And there are mere

trickles, like Jean Rhys. All that matters is feeding the lake. I don't matter. The lake matters. You must keep feeding the lake.[1]

Feeding the lake means that each of us takes our particular gift or talent and offers it to the world. In 1 Corinthians 12, the apostle Paul compares the church to the human body. In the church, there are many gifts and abilities, he says, and they are all necessary if the church is to do its work as the body of Christ. One person is the eye, one the ear, one the nose. And each person must contribute his or her unique gift to make the body function well.

That analogy is true not only for the church but also for the world. If the kingdom of God ever becomes a reality here on earth, it will be because everyone is feeding the lake. Everyone is creating something and bringing it to the world, so that the world becomes a collection of loving sacrifices and personal offerings of creativity. That may not happen any time soon, but wouldn't it be wonderful if it did?

Frankly, though, we have no control over what other people do. Our responsibility—indeed, our calling as people of God—is to contribute our part. Write our books. Compose our poems. Bake our bread. Paint our pictures. Bring our particular gift, as small and trivial as it may seem, and offer it for the building of that kingdom. Our calling is simply to feed the lake, to make our small offering to the world.

Creativity is an act of obedience to God. It might seem to be a stretch to claim that the stool we fashioned in the workshop or the dress we stitched on the sewing machine are, in reality, acts of obedience to God. But if they are done to feed the lake, and if they are an expression of who we are and what we love, that's exactly what they are.

In her book *Walking on Water*, Madeleine L'Engle wrote,

Obedience is an unpopular word nowadays, but the artist must be obedient to the work, whether it be a symphony, a painting, or a

---

1. Quoted in Madeleine L'Engle, *Walking on Water* (New York: Bantam Books, 1982), 23.

story for a small child. I believe that each work of art, whether it is a work of great genius, or something very small, comes to the artist and says, "Here I am. Enflesh me. Give birth to me." And the artist either says, "My soul doth magnify the Lord," and willingly becomes a bearer of the work or refuses . . . .[2]

We get those invitations frequently, if we have ears to hear them. We get silent invitations to create something that only we can create and then offer that creation as a gift to the world and to God. And, as Madeleine L'Engle said, when those invitations come, we're either obedient to them or we refuse them. God beckons to us in many strange ways, and one of them is the surprising, unspoken invitation to take the risk of creating.

The writer Bruce Lockerbie once wrote, "To serve Jesus Christ as an artist means offering to my Lord something that only I can give him—my own particular gift."[3] On our more faithful days, we say yes to those divine invitations to create, and we offer to God and the world what only we can give them—our own particular gift.

Finally, creativity calls for craftsmanship. Years ago, I came across a line that has both indicted me and inspired me since I heard it. I think it was spoken or written by Elton Trueblood, the Quaker writer and theologian. What he said was, "Holy shoddy is still shoddy."

By that, I think he meant that even if we're preaching a biblical sermon, singing or composing a hymn, or teaching a Bible class, we shouldn't assume that subject trumps style, that the "what" negates the importance of the "how." Just because the subject is "religious" doesn't mean we shouldn't worry about craftsmanship. In truth, because the subject is religious, we should be even *more* concerned about craftsmanship.

That means that every time we create something, we write it, paint it, compose it, build it, or cook it with a perfectionism that derives from caring. If we genuinely care about what we're creating, we'll refuse to do shoddy work.

---

2. L'Engle, *Walking on Water*, 18.

3. Bruce Lockerbie, *The Timeless Moment* (Westchester, IL: Cornerstone Books, 1980), 119.

Robert Capon once wrote,

> Culture can come only from caring enough about things to want
> them really to be themselves—to want the poem to scan perfectly,
> the song to be genuinely melodic, the basketball actually to drop
> through the middle of the hoop, the edge of the board to be utterly
> straight, the pastry to be really flaky. Few of us have many great
> things to care about, but we all have plenty of small ones.[4]

We all have plenty of small things to create, too. So let's roll up our
sleeves, fire up the computer, sharpen the tools, tune up the instru-
ment, or whatever else we need to do to fashion our personal offering
to God and the world. And let's care enough about that offering to
give it our best effort.

Let the poet wrestle with the words until the poem scans perfectly.
Let the musician struggle with the song until it is genuinely melodic.
Let the athlete keep shooting until the basketball drops squarely
through the middle of the hoop. Let the carpenter keep toiling until
the edge of the board is utterly straight. And let the chef keep fine-
tuning the recipe until the pastry is really flaky. Let us all care enough
about what we're creating to offer God and the world the best gift
we can bring.

Not only does the Bible begin with a creation story; it ends with
one, too. At the end of the book of Revelation, John sees a new
heaven and a new earth being created. He also sees the holy city, the
new Jerusalem, coming down from heaven from God, prepared as
a bride adorned for her husband. Overseeing all of this is God, the
one seated on the throne, who announces triumphantly, "See, I am
making all things new" (Rev 21:5a).

So at the beginning of the world, God is creating. And at the end
of the world, God is still creating. You can't help but think that God
loves to create and takes great delight in bringing new things into
being. You also can't help but think that we humans, created in God's

---

4. Robert Capon, *Bed and Board* (New York: Simon & Schuster, 1965),
108–109.

image, are supposed to create as well. Like the One who created us, we are to take our gifts and talents, as small and paltry as they may seem, and dare to whisper, "Behold, I make all things new."

Chapter 16

Words Matter
Choosing to Hurt or Heal

Because even the smallest of words can be the ones to hurt you, or save you. —Natsuki Tayaka

It hurts me to confess this, but in the spirit of honesty and transparency I feel that I should: I once committed a crime. I'm not proud of it and regret it, but it happened, and I can't erase it. So I need to tell you about it.

It happened when I was in the fifth grade. One Saturday morning, Eddie McGoodwin and I decided to climb up on the roof of our school, Ridgecrest Elementary. We had no sinister intentions at all; we wanted to see what the world looked like from that vantage point.

And the view was quite impressive. I could see my house on Turquoise Lane. I could see the houses of some of my friends. I could see Landrum Junior High. I could see cars passing by on the streets below. I could see the police car cruising by the school. I could see it turn into the school. I could see the policeman get out of his patrol car. I could see him motion for us to come down from the rooftop. And I could feel my heart start to sink.

When we got down to the patrol car, the policeman had a scowl on his face. He gruffly told us to get in the back seat and proceeded to read us the riot act. We had done something illegal, he said. We were guilty of a crime called "mischievous misdemeanor," and he would be reporting our crime to the school principal the next day.

I went home and tearfully told my parents what had happened. They didn't seem to be as devastated as I was, but I was inconsolable. I didn't know what "mischievous misdemeanor" was, but it sounded serious. It sounded like something that would warrant a long prison term, perhaps even an execution. I was ten years old, and I was a criminal.

I slept little that night and dreaded going to school the next day. But I got up and went and, sure enough, an announcement came over the intercom in our class that morning. "Would Jud Edwards please report to the principal's office immediately," a stern voice said. I made my way to the office of Mrs. Sculley, our principal, feeling like a convict marching to the guillotine.

I sat in a chair in front of Mrs. Sculley's desk. She asked me what had happened, and I told her that Eddie and I had climbed up on the school roof but that we didn't intend to do anything wrong, that we wanted to look around. I told her I was sorry and it would never happen again.

She looked at me . . . and smiled. She said she knew I was a good boy and believed me when I said we meant no harm. She said she had known me since I was in kindergarten and knew I had a good heart. But she said that I had made a mistake and it would probably be a good idea not to get on the school roof again. Then she told me to go back to class and not to worry about it anymore. I didn't walk back to class; I skipped. Mrs. Sculley had given me my life back again.

One of the things I learned from that experience, even as a ten-year-old, was that words have tremendous power. The policeman's words had the power to scare and dishearten me, to keep me awake at night, to bring tears to my eyes. Words, I had experienced firsthand, can *hurt*. But Mrs. Sculley's words had power, too—the power to restore my hope, to enable me to sleep in peace, to motivate me to skip down the hallway. Words, I had also experienced firsthand, can *heal*.

Perhaps no one better captures the paradoxical power of words than James in his epistle in the New Testament. He uses two metaphors to depict this power. Our words, he says, are like a rudder on a ship and like a fire. Are rudders and fires good things or bad things? Well, it all depends on how they're used. A rudder can guide a ship to safety, or it can lead a ship to disaster. A fire can warm a home and cook a meal, or it can destroy a home and burn a meal. Rudders and fires are neither good nor bad. It all depends on how people use them.

I've witnessed many occasions when words led to shipwreck and destructive infernos, times when words were used to *hurt*. Husbands and wives being critical of one another. Parents screaming at children. Preachers terrifying worshipers. Coaches intimidating athletes. We've all seen the awful damage words can do to relationships. And many times, the people hurling those destructive words at others are simply unaware of the damage they're causing. They're just words, right?

No, they're not *just* words. They're rudders that can lead a relationship to wreck and ruin. They're fires that can burn a relationship to the ground. We somehow need to recover the old Hebrew concept of words. James's metaphors of rudders and fires are much in the spirit of the ancient Hebrews in the Old Testament. They used a different metaphor, but it carried the same connotation. They believed that words are like arrows. Once words are fired into the air, they can't be retrieved. So, before you flippantly pick up that bow and shoot that arrow, they warned, count the possible cost. It has the power to wound, and even kill.

When I was a child we had a saying we would use when anyone fired one of those mean-spirited arrows at us. We would say, "Sticks and stones may break my bones, but words will never hurt me." Even as we said it, though, we knew it wasn't true. We knew that those words could wound us terribly because we had been wounded by them before. Words can hurt, and nearly all of us bear the scars that prove it.

But, thank God, that's not the whole story. Words can also *heal*. The rudder can guide the ship to harbor and safety. The fire can bake the bread and warm the house. "Words fitly spoken are like apples of gold in pictures of silver" (Prov 25:11, KJV), the writer of Proverbs says. Words fitly spoken can bring love to the loveless, joy to the joyless, hope to the hopeless, and resurrection to ten-year-old boys. If we sometimes underestimate the *damage* words can cause, we also sometimes underestimate the *delight* words can bring.

I'm sure Mrs. Sculley didn't think she was doing anything remarkable when she spoke to me in her office sixty years ago. She had no idea that she was making such an impact on my life or that I would remember her words years later and even write about them in a book. She was just doing her job as principal of Ridgecrest Elementary School. But her words were more enduring and influential than she ever could have imagined. And when I think back on them now, I wonder what it was about those words that made them so enduring and so powerful. As I ponder them now, I think it was because they were *personal, positive,* and *gracious.*

They were *personal* words because Mrs. Sculley knew me. I had been a student at her school since kindergarten. She knew my name, spoke to me in the hall nearly every day, had met my parents, and had a relationship with all of us. The lone ray of light in my dark world when I left my harrowing encounter with the policeman was this: he said he was going to report me to Mrs. Sculley. If Mrs. Sculley was going to be my judge and jury, I thought I might have a chance.

The most powerful, persuasive words we will ever speak will be spoken to people we know—our husband or wife, our children and grandchildren, our coworkers and fellow church members, our friends and neighbors. We know and love these people, and they know and love us, which gives us a credibility and intimacy we don't have anywhere else. That's why it's so crucial that we use our words to build them up and not to tear them down. That's why we need to be careful before we flippantly or angrily unleash our arrows into the air.

One of the things we notice when we read the New Testament is how personal most of Paul's letters are. He was writing to churches he had established and to people he knew well. He had an intimacy with them that gave him credibility and influence. So he measured his words carefully and used his influence to encourage and comfort those early Christians. And even when he had a correction or complaint to offer, he did it in the spirit of a loving parent. A word fitly spoken is a personal word addressed to people we know and love.

Mrs. Sculley's words were also *positive.* I think many school principals might have joined that policeman in reading me the riot act. She could have berated me and chastised me for breaking the rules.

She could have raised her voice and tried to intimidate me. But, bless her heart, she took the positive road. She said she knew I was a good boy and that I had meant no harm. She was *for* me, and I knew immediately that I was in the presence of kindness.

I know that some situations call for tough love. And I know that punishment is sometimes deserved and necessary. But it seems to me that tough love and punishment should be last resorts, not standard procedure. Standard procedure should be to expect the best in people and then to give them the opportunity to prove us right.

Finally, Mrs. Sculley's words were *gracious*. As I left the principal's office that day, her final words to me were, "Don't worry about it anymore." You can only imagine how relieved I was when I heard those words. I was absolved. There would be no prison sentence. Not even a detention hall. I was free to go. To collect baseball cards, sit in the Big Tree, toss the football around with my friends, and do all the other things ten-year-old boys do. Her parting words set me free to be a happy boy again.

The theological word for what she did that day is grace. Mrs. Sculley gave me grace. Grace happens any time someone conveys to us, "Don't worry about it anymore." Wouldn't it be wonderful if we could do that for the people in our lives? Give them grace instead of judgment? Set them free from worry instead of giving them reason to worry? Use our words as tools of freedom instead of weapons of punishment? Say to them, both verbally and nonverbally, "Don't worry about it anymore"?

I think the reason words of grace are so powerful is that they are so rare. Our culture is no friend to grace. We know all about climbing ladders, suffering consequences, pulling our weight, getting knocked around by life, and being criticized. But we know little about grace. So, when a Mrs. Sculley tells us not to worry about it, we're either skeptical, flabbergasted, or thrilled.

I can tell you from firsthand experience, though, that sometimes grace is really real. And giving it to the people in our lives is the finest thing we can do for them. It might even make them skip down the hallway.

It would be interesting to know how many words most of us have spoken or written in our lives. Those of us who like the sound of our own voices have probably spoken millions of words. And those of us who like the way we put words on paper have written thousands more. I think it's fair to say that those words have determined the kinds of lives we've lived. They've affected our relationships, our happiness, our vocational lives, and even our physical, emotional, and spiritual health. In a very real way, we are the sum of our words.

That's why words *matter*. They not only reveal who we are; they determine who we become. So I propose that we all take our cue from Mrs. Sculley and use words that are *personal, positive,* and *gracious.* Let's use our words to guide the ship to harbor and to warm some cold hearts. And let's never, ever fire an arrow without thinking about where that arrow might land.

Any talk of grace begins and ends with the way God has chosen to relate to us. So maybe I should spend the next chapter celebrating with you the amazing grace we have received from God.

Chapter 17

Grace Matters
Accepting God's Acceptance

I wanted to recover the kind of faith that has nothing to do with being sure what I believe and everything to do with trusting God to catch me though I am not sure of anything. —Barbara Brown Taylor

Once upon a time, long ago and far away, there lived a young Jewish rabbi named Saul. He was a zealous religious leader, intent on bringing the truth about God to the world around him. He was so zealous that he pursued and punished anyone who didn't believe the sacred truth of his forefathers.

Saul was so bright and so ambitious that he quickly advanced up the religious ladders of his day and became a rising rabbinical star. And he did all the right things to make that rise happen—study under the best teachers, make the best grades in his class, deliver eloquent speeches, and write erudite papers. His résumé was impressive, to say the least. Saul was on his way up, and he knew it.

But then something miraculous and inexplicable happened. While taking a trip to Damascus to round up infidels, he had an experience that turned his life upside down. He saw a light from the sky, was struck blind, fell to the ground, and heard a voice from heaven. He had no idea what was happening and neither did those around him. His traveling companions led him to Damascus, where he spent three long days and nights in the darkness without eating or drinking a thing.

It was a terrifying, outside-the-box experience, and from that moment forward young rabbi Saul would never be the same person. He would go away for three years to think about that experience and try to decide what it meant. And what he eventually decided was that, there on the road to Damascus, the God of the universe had rebooted his life. In his old life as a rising rabbinical star, Saul had been in charge—studying the Torah, writing the papers, making the grades, defending the truth, climbing the ladder of ministerial success, and ridding the world of heretics.

But what Saul would eventually conclude was that on the road to Damascus, God had given him a whole new operating system. In this new operating system, Saul would not be in charge; God would. After all, nothing that had happened on that road was Saul's doing. He was not in charge of anything. He was simply the recipient of a bunch of bewildering events that fell completely beyond his training and expertise. Probably for the first time in his high-achieving life, Saul was at the mercy of events he neither expected, orchestrated, nor deserved.

So Saul the rabbi, operating under a system of works and law, became Paul the apostle, operating under a new system of grace and freedom. And he became convinced that his frightening experience on the road to Damascus was the best thing that had ever happened to him. He would go on to write a series of letters detailing to others the breathtaking advantages of this new grace system God had given him. Perhaps this section from his letter to the Ephesians sums up his new operating system as well as any: "For by grace you have been saved through faith, and this is not your own doing; it is the gift of God—not the result of works, so that no one may boast. For we are what he has made us, created in Christ Jesus for good works, which God prepared beforehand to be our way of life" (Eph 2:8-9).

The conversion of the apostle Paul on the Damascus road has become one of the most famous conversions in history. And many of us are envious of that experience and wish we could have one like it ourselves. During my first year at seminary, I once sat in a recliner in my living room and asked God to give me a dramatic experience like Paul had. "God, if you will just give me an experience like Paul's," I prayed, "I will never doubt you. If you will come out in the open and reveal yourself to me, I will be as bold and committed as he was." I waited for three hours in that recliner, and nothing happened. No lights. No voices. No nothing.

I got up from the recliner knowing that, for reasons known only to God, I wouldn't get Paul's kind of conversion experience. I would have to be content with a quieter, less dramatic divine encounter that would require more faith than lights and voices would.

Thank God, I did, like Paul, eventually find a new operating system by which to run my life—the same operating system of grace he discovered on that fateful journey to Damascus. As I mentioned earlier, my first steps of faith were steeped in fear, guilt, and attempts to win the favor of God through good works. I was determined to be a 100-percent Christian, and my weekly offering envelope would prove it to anyone who cared enough to notice.

Sometime in my twenties, though, I started to embrace a grace-oriented theology that made me understand for the first time that the word "gospel" means good news. I started to realize that when the Bible says we love God because God *first* loved us, it means exactly that. God loved me before I ever prayed a prayer, witnessed to a friend, did my daily Bible readings, went to a church service, or put money in an offering envelope.

For anyone who has grown up as a checklist Christian, struggling to earn God's favor through a long series of good deeds, that is incredibly good news. When you've spent a lifetime trying to climb the ladder of goodness to win God's approval, it's a great relief to learn that you can finally quit climbing, that you already have God's favor.

Once we, like rabbi Saul, reboot and move from the operational system of works to the operational system of grace, we start to notice over time the enormous benefits of this new system. Getting out of the works system and into the grace system brings some wonderful rewards. Let me recount just a few of them.

For one thing, grace produces gratitude. After all, what is the most natural response to a gift? It's gratitude, because someone has seen fit to bestow upon us something we neither earned nor deserved. Only an ingrate would fail to be thankful for a precious gift.

As I write this, I'm thinking now of two of the old hymns I grew up singing at church. One is "Amazing Grace," the most famous song about grace ever written. John Newton wrote that hymn as a way to express his gratitude to God for rescuing him from a life of serious sin. Remember how the hymn begins? "Amazing grace, how sweet the sound that saved a wretch like me. I once was lost but now am found. Was blind but now I see."

What do you do when you are a wretch headed for ruin and Someone saves you? What do you do when you are lost and Someone finds you? And what do you do when you are blind and Someone restores your sight? Well, what you do is break out in a song of gratitude. You have been given some unspeakably wonderful gifts, and the only sane response is to break out in a heartfelt song of thanksgiving for the amazing grace you've received.

The other old song I'm remembering is not as famous as "Amazing Grace," but it is filled with just as much gratitude. In the hymn "Showers of Blessing," the chorus exults about "showers of blessing, showers of blessing we need. Mercy drops 'round us are falling. But for the showers we plead." Notice what kind of drops are falling: *mercy* drops. Grace is falling everywhere, but the writer pleads for showers of it. You can never get too much grace, and you can never be too thankful for it when it arrives.

Should we ever forget how amazing grace is or how much grace we're being showered with, all we need to do is stop and remember how many gifts we receive on a daily basis. Did we do anything to create or deserve the air we breathe, the water we drink, the sunshine that gives us warmth, the trees that give us shade, or the birds that sing in our backyard? Did we do anything to control the earth spinning at just the right speed at just the right distance from the sun? Those are all gifts we receive every day, and we shouldn't ever take them for granted.

Did we create the eyes with which we see our wonderful world, the ears with which we hear those birds singing in the backyard, or the nose with which we smell that homemade bread coming out of the oven? Did we create the cat that curls up in our lap every evening or the cows that graze in the fields? The list of things we did *not* create or produce is so long it's almost endless. Suffice it to say, we're not just getting drops of mercy; we're getting showers of blessing on a daily basis. If we're attentive at all, we see grace everywhere.

And since that is true in the realm of creation, why shouldn't it also be true in the realm of the spirit? Why should we be surprised that our salvation, our standing with God, is a function of grace as well? If God has gifted us with an endless list of *natural* gifts, why should it shock us that God has also gifted us with an endless list of *spiritual* gifts?

That's the discovery Paul made there on the road to Damascus and the gift he celebrated all of his life. As he celebrated with the Ephesians, our very salvation comes by grace. It is not of ourselves; it is the gift of God, not of works lest any of us should boast. Just as we can't produce the air that keeps us alive, so we can't produce the salvation that puts us right with God.

That's why grace always produces gratitude. We've been given a priceless gift—the love and acceptance of God. And we get to spend the rest of our lives breathing the fresh air of freedom and joy. When we experience amazing grace and feel those refreshing showers of blessing, gratitude comes easy.

But grace doesn't just make us grateful; it also makes us more gracious in our relationships with others. Grace, in other words, produces grace. The people who have received the grace of God become bestowers of grace on the people around them.

One of my all-time favorite parables of Jesus is the parable of the laborers in the vineyard in Matthew 20:1-16. It's not one of his most famous parables, but it has a truth in it about grace that we dare not miss. In the story, a landowner hires workers at different times of the day to work in his vineyard—some early in the morning, some at nine, noon, and three, and a final group just an hour before quitting time. At the end of the day, the landowner gathers them together to hand out the paychecks . . . and surprisingly pays them all the same amount.

Those who have worked all day are incensed. How could the landowner be so unfair? They have toiled all day in the hot sun, while the latecomers just sashayed in at quitting time and got the same pay. In the parable, Jesus says these upset laborers "grumbled" at the inequity of it all. And who can blame them? Every labor union in the world would be on their side.

But the landowner holds his ground. He reminds them that he had agreed to pay them a day's wages, and he has been true to his word. What he did for the other workers was none of their business. The story ends with the landowner asking, "Am I not allowed to do what I choose with what belongs to me? Or are you so envious because I am generous?" (Matt 20:35).

The reason I like that parable so much is because it makes it clear that we have a distinct choice in our approach to life: we can choose to be people of the early morning, or we can choose to be people of the late afternoon. And that choice will determine the kind of attitude we have and, for all practical purposes, the kind of life we will lead.

If we choose to be people of the early morning, we'll do a lot of "grumbling." We'll see ourselves as faithful, hard-working people who've never gotten what we've deserved. We'll position ourselves as victims and believe that God, life, and people are not fair. Mostly, we'll go through life angry and judgmental because others, not nearly as deserving, seem to be getting all the breaks. People of the early morning know a lot about works and almost nothing about grace.

People of the late afternoon, on the other hand, can't believe how blessed they are. They showed up at quitting time and got the whole day's pay! They know they've gotten far more than they deserve and go through life shaking their heads in wonder at their remarkable fate. Because God, life, and people have been so absurdly generous to them, they're absurdly generous to others. People of the late afternoon have received so much grace that they can't help but give it away.

That's the second reason grace matters so much. Not only does it make us grateful; it also makes us gracious. People who believe in and have experienced grace are filled with gratitude, and that gratitude makes them more loving and forgiving in their relationships with others.

The third reason grace is so vital to our lives is that it gives us confidence when life starts to collapse all around us. On those days when the sun refuses to shine and hope seems to be on permanent hiatus, it is the grace of God that can get us through the darkness. On those dark days, we find ourselves affirming with Paul, "If God is for us, who can be against us?" (Rom 8:31, KJV).

Lewis Smedes once wrote a book he titled *How Can It Be All Right When Everything Is All Wrong?* In that book, he depicted a dark time in his own life that he described like this:

> I had never known such lonely pain, never such fear, never such helplessness, never such despair. I was lost, utterly lost. I felt a life of pious trying going down the drain, a life of half-baked belief in grace exposed as futile. I was sunk. I screamed for help, and none could come. I was making my bed in hell.[1]

But what he discovered, to his great relief, was that God would be in that hell with him:

> I discovered, all by myself, in touch only with my final outpost of feeling, that I could be left, deserted, alone, all my scaffolds knocked down, all the stanchions beneath me pulled away, my buttresses fallen, I could be stripped of human hands, and I could survive. In my deepest heart, I survived, stood up, stayed whole, held by nothing at all but the grace of a loving God.[2]

What Lewis Smedes discovered, I think, is that the grace of God is real. It's not just a theological concept. It's not just wishful thinking. It's not just something preachers preach about in sermons. It's as real as the love you have for your children or the joy you feel when they succeed at some difficult task. It's as real as the devotion you have for your husband or wife or the satisfaction you get from serving others.

---

1. Lewis Smedes, *How Can It Be All Right When Everything Is All Wrong?* (San Francisco: Harper & Row, 1982), 115.
2. Smedes, *How Can It Be All Right*, 115.

And when grace is tested, it holds. It works. If, like Lewis Smedes, we are held by nothing at all but the grace of a loving God, that's enough to hold us for an eternity.

The final reason grace matters so much is that it enables us to relax. Since God is *for* us, since God loves us unconditionally, since God has already accepted us in Christ, and since we can't do one more thing to make God love us more, we can breathe a huge sigh of relief . . . and relax. We can quit being like the elder brother in the parable of the prodigal son and decide instead to come to the party.

We can choose to become one of the people of the late afternoon and revel in the goodness of God and the wonder of life. We can quit being so uptight and antiseptic and laugh a little more. We can become like the anonymous friar in a Nebraska monastery who wrote:

> If I had my life to live over, I'd try to make more mistakes next time. I would relax, I would limber up, I would be sillier than I was this trip. I know of very few things I would take seriously. I would be less hygienic. I would take more chances. I would take more trips. I would climb more mountains, swim more rivers, and watch more sunsets. I would eat more ice cream. I would have more actual troubles and fewer imaginary ones.[3]

I'm afraid that this monk and I are kindred spirits. Like him, I've lived sanely and sensibly all of my days. Like him, I've worried too much and laughed too little. But, like him, I'm working on it. And grace is my best ally in this quest to relax more and experience what Jesus called "life more abundant."

Once grace seeps down into the depths of our soul, we get the three attributes I've already delineated: a spirit of gratitude, a more gracious attitude toward others, and confidence that we can make it through anything. But we also get the capacity to relax and hang a little looser. If we're loved and accepted by God just as we are, the

---

3. Quoted in John Killinger, *Bread for the Wilderness, Wine for the Journey* (Waco: Word Books, 1976), 69.

pressure to perform is gone. We're free to relax and relish the incredible grace of God.

Once rabbi Saul had his experience on the road to Damascus and got a new operating system, he discovered all four of the things I've just mentioned. He not only discovered those truths but also began writing letters to the early churches to make sure they knew those truths as well. Paul became the great proponent and defender of grace in the ancient world.

One time he heard about some churches in Galatia that were abandoning the grace system and going back to the old works system. He could hardly believe it and told those Galatian Christians, in no uncertain terms, that they were making a huge mistake: "I am astonished that you are so quickly deserting the one who called you in the grace of Christ and are turning to a different gospel . . ." (Gal 1:6).

He uses the Galatian letter to remind them of the advantages of the grace system and offers this analogy: "For freedom Christ has set us free. Stand firm, therefore, and do not submit again to a yoke of slavery" (Gal 5:1). Under the old operating system of works, you were in slavery, Paul told them. In slavery to checking boxes, climbing ladders, and earning brownie points. But when you found the new operating system of grace, you were delivered from that bondage and set free so you could live with gratitude. Set free so you could treat others with grace. Set free so you could have confidence on even your darkest days. Set free so you could relax into the acceptance of God.

Why, he asks them, would you want to forfeit all of that and return to the old operating system that was making you miserable? Why would you choose the slavery of the works system over the freedom of the grace system?

It was a good question when Paul posed it over two thousand years ago, and it's still a good question today.

Chapter 18

Memories Matter
Discovering Gratitude and Hope

*Your memory is the glue that binds your life together;
everything you are today is because of your amazing
memory. You are a data collecting being, and your
memory is where your life is lived.* —Kevin Horsley

I still remember my Nocona baseball glove. I had been dreaming
about that glove for months and riding my bike to Slater Martin
Sporting Goods on Long Point Road just to look at it, try it on,
and dream of one day owning it. But it seemed like an impossible
dream because the glove was expensive, and I didn't have any money.
My parents weren't exactly rich either. So the possibility of me ever
owning that Nocona glove seemed remote, to say the least.

Our family had a tradition of having Easter chairs every year on
Easter Sunday. My brother, sister, and I each had our own chair on
which our parents usually put some candy, an Easter outfit to wear,
and a toy of some kind. I guess you could say it was our family's
version of a Christmas stocking at Easter.

You can probably guess where this story is going. On the Easter
I'm remembering, I entered the living room, went to my Easter chair,
and was amazed to see that Nocona glove I'd been dreaming about
for months. I don't know if I've ever been as surprised or delighted
by a gift as I was that Easter morning. A Nocona glove. Of my own.
Just for me. To assure I'd make the big leagues.

That was about sixty years ago, and I remember it like it was
yesterday. I'm sure my mom and dad had no idea I would remember
that occasion sixty years later or that I would one day write about it

in a book. But some memories—and we're not always sure which ones—last a lifetime.

When I read back over what I've written in these pages, I'm surprised at some of the memories I decided to include. I've subtitled this book "Looking Back on a Life of Joy," and the things I've remembered as I've looked back are not exactly earth-shattering or dramatic:

- miniature golf with grandsons
- checking the boxes on an offering envelope
- Nerf basketball games
- S&H Green Stamps
- Norm Bulaich
- running a marathon
- my first royalty check
- Bronc Burnett and Chip Hilton
- a phone conversation with my sister
- Tim Conway and Don Knotts
- The Gold Dust Twins
- Don Williams
- The Big Tree
- Walden Pond
- "project" kits
- pecan pies
- Mr. Bayh
- Mrs. Sculley
- a Nocona baseball glove

I'm not sure there's one thing on that list that is headline material or particularly life-changing. These seem like insignificant footnotes, not the defining moments of a person's life. And yet, for some reason, these are the memories that washed ashore when I was looking back on the things that have brought me joy. If nothing else, this list reminds me that "little things" are not so little after all. And that memories—even the little ones—are important. Memories *matter*, I think, because of what they bring to our lives.

For one thing, they make us grateful. In the last chapter, I suggested that grace makes us grateful, and I'm convinced that memories do, too. The word "remember" appears over 150 times in the Bible. Over and over, people in Scripture are admonished to remember God, remember the commandments, remember the sabbath day to keep it holy, remember what God has done in the past, remember the patriarchs, remember to take care of the poor. Remember. Remember. Remember.

And to make sure they remembered, the Jews in the Old Testament did two things. First, they put phylacteries on their foreheads and wrists so they would never forget the actions and commandments of God. These actions and commandments were so vital that they never wanted to run the risk of forgetting them. Second, they erected stones and monuments to commemorate where significant events had occurred. That way, every time they saw these stones and monuments, they would remember what God had done for them at that place.

The ultimate purpose of both practices was to remind the people to be grateful for what God had done for them in the past. When they wore those phylacteries and erected those stones, the people were remembering what God had done for them and reminding themselves to be grateful for their history. They were using their memory to stir up gratitude.

We Christians don't wear phylacteries anymore, but we do still erect stones and monuments to mark significant events and places. Every time we visit a grave site or see a war memorial, we're reminded to be grateful for the people and events those markers represent. And nearly all of us take pictures, stuff them in albums, and take them out occasionally to remember significant moments in our lives. The weddings, birthday parties, ball games, and other momentous occasions are all catalogued in those picture albums or maybe sent out to the world on Facebook or Instagram. Every one of those pictures and postings is an expression of gratitude.

So memories matter because they make us grateful. If we're honest we also have to admit that we have memories that make us sad or regretful, too. No one's memory bank has only positive experiences in it. For too many people, memories are something to forget, not remember. But for most of us, the good memories far outnumber the bad. And every time we do what I've done in these pages and take a walk down memory lane, we find ourselves whispering a prayer of gratitude for the people and experiences in our lives.

Because memories have a way of making us grateful, they also have a way of making us hopeful. After all, if God has blessed us with such wonderful people and experiences in the past, won't God also bless us with wonderful people and experiences in the future? When Paul wrote his friends in Philippi, he said to them, "I am confident of this, that the one who began a good work among you will bring it to completion by the day of Jesus Christ" (Phil 1:6). The One who began a good work in their lives would not abandon or forsake them; God would see them all the way to the finish line.

I do not for a moment believe that my list of good memories is finished. I'm hoping and trusting that the God who began a good work in me, the God who has blessed me immeasurably throughout my life, still has some blessings left for me. When I survey my past, in other words, I'm filled with hope for my future.

There was a time in the nation of Israel when, after trudging through the wilderness for forty long years, they finally made it to the promised land. As they often did, they decided to erect a monument at Gilgal, where they entered the land of Canaan. At the dedication service of the Gilgal memorial, Joshua told the people to use these stones as a reminder of the way God had led them and even performed miracles to make that day possible. Every time they saw those stones, they were to remember the providence of God.

Haven't we all been through times when we thought we might not make it? Times when we were carrying some burden we thought might be too heavy? Times when we were dealing with some crisis that seemed overwhelming? Times when, like those ancient Israelites, we were trudging through some awful wilderness?

But then, some amazing things happened. Or maybe just some ordinary things happened. We found surprising strength. We experienced an unusual sense of the presence of God in that situation. Surprising doors opened, and unexpected events occurred. And, wonder of wonders, we got through that wilderness and made it to the promised land.

If we were smart, we erected some kind of monument in our minds on the far shore of that trauma. We filed that experience in our memory so that we could go back to it should we ever find ourselves in another wilderness. And when we have to deal with another crisis, we can find hope and declare that the God who saw us through that first wilderness experience will also see us through this one. The gratitude we felt in that first wilderness will give us hope for all the future wildernesses we have to endure.

So our memories give us hope. We get to look back with gratitude at all of the blessings we've received and then have the hope that the God of those blessings is still in the blessing business. The One who began a good work in us will get us victoriously to the finish line.

There's an old joke that's not as funny to me now as it used to be. A man went to his doctor and said, "Doc, I have a real problem. I can't remember a thing." The doctor said, "How long have you had this problem?" And the man said, "What problem?"

The older I get, the less funny that joke becomes. But as long as I have a memory at all, I will try to use it to be grateful and to be hopeful. Perry Como once had a hit song that went, "Catch a falling star and put it in your pocket; save it for a rainy day." Good memories are like falling stars that we can catch and put in our pockets and save for a rainy day. And then, when the winds blow and the rains come, we can take out a memory . . . and find both gratitude and hope.

As I look back over what I've written in these pages, I'm struck by two things. First, I'm struck by how many things I *didn't* include on my list of things that matter. Anyone reading this book could justifiably wonder why other things didn't make the list. Doesn't friendship matter? Doesn't prayer matter? How about money and health? What about the church? What about barbecue, for goodness' sake? Don't those things matter? All I can say in my defense is that space constraints prevented me from including everything that could have been in the book. If the book flies off the shelves and the publisher begs for a sequel, I'd be happy to write one: *Panning for More Gold.* I'm keenly aware that what matters to me might not matter to others. Each one of us could compile our own unique list of what matters to us, and no two of those lists would be the same. I would like to think that some of the items on my list have intersected with some of the items on your list and that we are, at least in a few crucial ways, kindred spirits.

But even if that's not the case, I hope this book will prompt you to think about what matters to you. The process of defining those things is crucial because pinpointing what has mattered to us in the *past* helps us define what we should focus on in the *future*. Once we've determined what has been wheat and what has been chaff in our lives, we can then start focusing on the wheat, the things that really matter to us.

In 1934, Admiral Richard Byrd wanted to establish a weather station deep in the Antarctic, near the South Pole. A team of hardy men was supposed to work with him on the project, but the team disintegrated, leaving Admiral Byrd to settle into his Boston-built hut by himself. He stayed there four and a half months, as the temperature outside plummeted to eighty-three degrees below zero.

It was a dark, cold, quiet, and lonely vigil, the kind of experience most people could not, and would not, endure. When Admiral Byrd came out of his frozen cocoon, people were anxious to hear what he had to say. Early on, he reported, he felt lost and depressed. But then he settled in and adjusted to the solitude. "My thoughts seemed to come together more smoothly than ever before," he said. "I am better able to tell what is wheat for me and what is chaff."

None of us will have an Admiral Byrd kind of experience— and, frankly, we have no desire to spend over four months in frozen solitary confinement. But what he gained from that experience is something we should seek while we can: deciding what is wheat and what is chaff in our lives and choosing to spend the rest of our days focusing on what really matters.

It is an exercise well worth the effort. It will likely fill us with gratitude as we count our many blessings. But it will also fill us with hope as we think about how we will spend the days in our future. Armed with gratitude and hope, we will step into that future with purpose and joy. And when we reach the end of that journey, we might even find ourselves echoing the dying words of the apostle Paul: "I have fought the good fight; I have finished the race; I have kept the faith" (2 Tim 4:7).

Have a good trip.